I CAN SEE WHAT YOUR BODY IS SAYING

An Introduction to Micro Expressions and Body Language and Their Energetic Connections

RODNEY SMITH

I Can See What Your Body Is Saying
An Introduction to Body Language and
Micro Expressions and Their Energetic Connections

Vision is the art of seeing what
is invisible to others.
~ JONATHAN SWIFT

CONTENTS

Dedication vii

Foreword ix

Chapter 1:   Why Is Any of This Important? 1

Chapter 2:   When There Is a Lack of SKILL 8

Chapter 3:   The Road Map to Success 16

Chapter 4:   The Mechanics of Reading Others 25

Chapter 5:   Understanding Energy and the Body 34

Chapter 6:   Micro Expression Basics 52

Chapter 7:   Body Language Basics 65

Chapter 8:   Understanding Combinations 98

Chapter 9:   How to See What the Body Is Saying 106

Chapter 10: Putting It All Together 112

Bibliography 119

About the Author 123

DEDICATION

This book is dedicated to my family and friends who have supported me throughout my life. I appreciate your kind words and advice to help me succeed and grow in each of my ventures in life. Without your encouragement, I would not have pushed myself to do many of the things I have done.

To my mom, thank you for teaching me to never give up and instilling within me the understanding that failure is not an option. It has been through observing you from my childhood to adulthood that I have learned to persevere in hard times and weather the storms. As a single mother of three, you have always provided for your children and showed us the true meaning of having fortitude during adverse times. I'm sure there were times when you felt like giving up, but you always managed to come out on top. You have been the perfect example of demonstrating kindness to others and maintaining professionalism even when others act in an unfair manner. You never doubted me in my dreams nor discouraged me from trying new or different things and have supported me in my endeavors. Thank you for always being there and sharing your knowledge with me when I needed you.

To my sisters, thank you both for being there in difficult times and being the ears that listened to the headaches and struggles I have faced. Thank you for showing me how to pursue goals, continuously try new things, and not be afraid to fail. I have seen each of you face new challenges in life head-on with little to no complaint. You have both been inspirations and demonstrated tremendous courage and fortitude despite the odds.

To my wife, thank you dearly for supporting everything I have ever desired to do. You have motivated and pushed me to be resilient. You have stood by my side through the good and challenging times and never doubted my ability to be successful. You have been my number one fan, cheerleader, promoter, and business partner. You have created opportunities to show my talents, skills, and abilities to others even when I did not want to because of my self-doubt, but they always worked out for the best. Thank you for never giving up on me and putting up with the late-night studying and researching to improve and become the best me you knew I could be. You have encouraged me to do things that I felt I would be a failure in and stood by my side each and every step of the way.

Finally, to my dad, thank you for the conversations we've had and the knowledge you gave me to help me grow and succeed. You enlightened me in areas I was lacking and showed me that it was OK to be emotional as a man and still have my pride. I saw firsthand the changes within you that illustrated that change for the better can and will happen if you believe. Thank you for your prayers and for illustrating that keeping the faith in tough times will bring brighter days. I will miss you dearly. Rest easy now as you have fought the good fight!

FOREWORD

Picture this: You stumble across this old, dusty map, right? But it's not your typical "X marks the spot" kind of deal. Nah, this map is all about unlocking the secrets to the human vibe, the real talk that our bodies are throwing out there when words just aren't cutting it. Enter my friend and fellow body language expert Rodney Smith, a seasoned navigator of the human condition (aka the real MVP of cracking the human code), who has spent years in the law enforcement trenches. He offers us his secrets he's used for decades on how to decode the silent whispers of suspects and witnesses alike. In his future New York Times best-selling epic book, "I Can See What Your Body is Saying," Rodney shares his very personal compass with us, allowing every reader, not just the seasoned detective, to understand the unspoken truths hidden in plain sight.

Now, Rodney isn't just any 'ole nice guy off the street. This guy's been in the thick of it, in law enforcement, where reading a room can mean the difference between cracking a case and hitting a dead end - and he happens to also be the nicest guy you'll ever meet! And what Rodney is giving you in this book is pure gold. It's like he's handing us all these secret decoder rings, transforming us from clueless bystanders to masters of the silent conversation happening right under our noses.

Our paths crossed in a manner as serendipitous as it was destined. My name is Janine Driver and I'm the CEO of the Body Language Institute and the author of the New York Times best-selling book, "You Say More Than You Think" and Washington Post best-seller "You Can't Lie to Me." I'm also the body language contributor to such networks as CourtTV, NBC, CNN, and FOX. Rodney and I originally met through his role as a law enforcement instructor, a calling that further cemented his expertise in the realm of non-verbal cues. He had stumbled upon my appearance with another detecting deception expert on a Discovery Channel documentary called, "Secrets of Interrogation." Evidentially, Rodney used that video in a course on body language and detecting deception in a law enforcement class he was teaching. This shared interest led Rodney to sign up for my online body language training, a decision that would mark the beginning of a significant and enduring friendship. Our first conversation in December 2019 was the spark that ignited a journey of mutual respect, learning, and mentorship that has enriched both our lives. Plus, now both Rodney and I weigh in on infamous criminal cases - together - on CourtTV with Vinnie Politan.

Now it's your turn to be trained by my dear friend and lead instructor at my company, BLI! Imagine hanging out with Rodney as he guides you through this jungle of non-verbal cues, from the subtle eyebrow twitch to the full-on energy vibes we're all throwing out there. It's a journey from "huh?" to "aha!" making the deep dive from "The Mechanics of Reading Others" to "Understanding Combinations," and finally hitting us with the grand finale, "Putting It All Together."

And here's the kicker: Rodney's not just talking to the badge-wearing heroes among us. This book? It's for everybody. Whether you're trying to navigate the daily grind or just looking to get a leg up on understanding your fellow humans, Rodney's breaking down those "keep out" signs and laying out the welcome mat.

Diving into "Understanding Energy and the Body," (my favorite part of this incredible book) Rodney hits us with this mind-blowing concept of linking up body language with chakras. Yeah, you heard that right. It's like he's spotted this hidden treasure that's been right in front of our eyes this whole time, but no one thought to look there. It's not just about what we're saying; it's about the whole energy field we're rocking.

So, why should you buy this book? Here are ten reasons that make "I Can See What Your Body is Saying" an indispensable guide to the world of non-verbal communication:

1. Discover the Unspoken: Learn to decode the silent messages we all send, enhancing your understanding of those around you.

2. Build Stronger Relationships: Use your new knowledge to connect on a deeper level with friends, family, and colleagues.

3. Gain a Competitive Edge: Apply body language insights in your professional life to negotiate, persuade, and lead more effectively.

4. Enhance Personal Safety: Recognize potential threats through subtle cues, keeping yourself and others safe.

5. Boost Confidence: Understanding and using body language effectively can increase your self-assurance in social situations.

6. Improve Communication Skills: Complement your verbal communication with the right non-verbal cues for clearer, more effective interactions.

7. Navigate Cultural Differences: Body language is universal. Learn the nuances to bridge gaps in cross-cultural communication.

8. Access Expert Knowledge: Benefit from Rodney's extensive experience in law enforcement and body language expertise.

9. Embark on a Journey of Self-Discovery: Reflect on your own body language and what it says about you.

10. Join a Community of Observers: Be part of a group that appreciates the power of non-verbal.

In conclusion, if you're ready to jump into this adventure, to crack the code of human interaction and become the Sherlock Holmes of body language, then what are you waiting for? Get your hands on this book. Let's dive into the magic of understanding each other without saying a word. Welcome to your new superpower with "I Can See What Your Body is Saying."

Let's make this journey legendary.

Janine Driver, President
The Body Language Institute & The Decision Profiling Group
www.LyinTamer.com

"We believe in looking at the world in a different way."

Chapter One

WHY IS ANY OF THIS IMPORTANT?

**The purpose of learning is growth, and
our minds, unlike our bodies, can continue
growing as we continue to live.**
~ MORTIMER ADLER

ebruary 14, 2002, was a day I'll never forget. First, it was Valentine's Day and I was single, but more importantly, it was the day I accepted a job offer to start my career in law enforcement. I reported to the police academy two weeks later for several months of training to prepare me for my new role as a police officer. From taking classes on ethics to learning how to interpret the laws and statutes, drive with precision, and perform defensive tactics, as well as qualifying with a handgun, I successfully graduated and began my field training shortly thereafter. I rode alongside a variety of veteran officers for the next four months who showed me the ropes of how to help others and not get myself hurt or killed in the process. I basically knew just enough to be dangerous as I was fresh and green as grass and had no real experience other than the training I had experienced weeks and months prior. I learned how to write reports, perform traffic stops, evaluate a person's statements to determine whether crimes had been committed, and a host of other tasks that would help determine whether I was ready to be released to solo patrol to work by myself.

Interestingly, in field training, I was never really taught how to read people other than to watch their hands as they could hit, strike, or carry weapons and use them against me. After all, it wasn't like I was some highly skilled fighter like Bruce Lee or Jason Bourne. Some behaviors that people would display came across as obvious, such as looking around nervously approached by law enforcement or leaving the area as soon as we arrived. Unfortunately, there were not any classes in the basic law enforcement training curriculum or in field training that delved deeply into analyzing statements and properly distinguishing truthful behaviors from nervous or deceptive ones. These were classes that had to be requested later as a part of continuing education. To be honest, in some respects, that wasn't a big deal at the time because it didn't seem necessary for my role as a patrol officer. If I clocked someone on the radar speeding, it didn't call for an in-depth interview. I had the evidence on the radar unit, and I would speak with the driver to get their side of the story, run a check on their license, and then make a determination to issue a warning or citation. If a house was broken into, I just needed to get the details of when it was last secured, when it was found broken into, what was taken, and then write the report. I felt just fine in doing those tasks, as I had been taught how to accomplish them. In some interactions with others, I would go with my gut feeling if something didn't seem right and look further if needed. As I reflect on my career, I often wonder how many times potential negative encounters passed me by and I was saved through grace and mercy in spite of my ignorance, lack of knowledge, and failure to recognize warning signs of danger.

Even as I look back at the previous jobs I've had in my life, no job ever trained me how to read or analyze the behavior of others. When I was a bagger at the grocery store, no one taught me how to recognize a thief. As a cook at a fast-food restaurant, I wasn't negotiating sales by getting customers to buy more food or determining whether they were honest in stating they wanted extra cheese on their sandwich. In other words, I was not involved in processes that required special skill in determining whether someone was lying. Basically, I was trained to do a specific task and ultimately, that's what I did. I have casually met people from all walks of life and different professions and told them what I do for a living. During those conversations, I might ask them if they have ever had any formal training in recognizing signs of truth or deception or even on the mechanics of reading and understanding others, and in almost every circumstance, the answer is no. Even as you are beginning to read this book, think about whether you have had specific training to read and analyze others as well. I also ask you to think about and answer the following questions:

- Have you ever been lied to?

- How did you feel once you found out someone had lied to you?

- More importantly, think of times you may have been deceived that you are still unaware of.

Every day, no matter where you are, if you are in the business of interacting with people, there is a strong chance you will be lied to during your daily interactions. Although some lies are harmless and simple forms of exaggeration or designed to prevent hurting another's feelings, not all lies or methods of deceit are created equal. Imagine investing your life savings, purchasing a product, or meeting someone you may be attracted to, only to find that the information you were told was false. How awesome would it be to not only sense that something doesn't feel right in your gut but be able to validate what you feel?

For decades, even centuries, scientists and researchers have searched for the ability to distinguish truth from deception. Many areas around the world had their own methods of lie detection. In India around 1500 BC, priests would test suspects by placing a donkey inside a dark tent and dipping its tail in soot from an oil lamp. The suspects were told there was a magic donkey inside the tent, and they were to go inside and pull on the donkey's tail. If they were innocent, nothing would happen, but if they were guilty, the donkey would bray. Once the suspects came out of the tent, their hands would be examined for soot. If their hands were dirty, they were presumed to be innocent, whereas if they were clean, they were deemed as guilty. The theory was that a guilty person would not want to chance pulling on the tail out of fear that the donkey would bray, so they would refrain from touching it altogether.

In China around 1000 BC, an early form of lie detection was to place dry grains of rice in a suspect's mouth when trying to obtain a confession of guilt. It was believed that if a suspect was guilty, their mouth would dry out and the rice they spit out would be dry as well. The rationale was that saliva would decrease during times of emotional anxiety. If the rice was wet after the suspect was questioned, the suspect was considered innocent as they evidently had plenty of saliva, giving the impression they were not nervous or under stress.

This holds true even today—we often see people get "cotton mouth" when nervous as the flow of saliva is restricted. Individuals may try to swallow or gulp, but it is difficult because they don't have enough saliva in their mouths. It is not uncommon to see a person wanting to drink water during questioning, especially after hot topic questions. This is somewhat like the effects of wanting water when dehydrated.

Unfortunately, no invention has ever been created that can detect lies— or the truth, for that matter. Even the polygraph, invented in 1921 by John Larson, still has its validity questioned. While the polygraph is a great tool for investigative purposes, it must be operated by an individual who monitors the candidate as the instrument measures and records their physiological responses. As with any piece of manufactured equipment, there is always opportunity for error. In some cases, false positives or negatives could suggest that an innocent person is guilty or vice versa.

Aside from lying and deception, the need to understand body language is important in our lives as it plays a huge part in our communication process. The ability to understand others while being self-aware is vital for our survival. Communication problems are huge when it comes to businesses losing money or employees, as well as personal relationships surviving disagreements due to misunderstanding. In business transactions, let's face it, we all want the best deal for our hard-earned money. No one ever wants to feel as though they have been taken for a ride and gypped in the process. The ability to understand unspoken communication is important for everyone as there are so many things that are not verbally stated but shown through actions.

I'm sure we can all think of a time when we were deceived and the imprint it left on us. Did it make you feel helpless? Angry? Betrayed? Maybe it left you with a sense of shock or disbelief as you realized what had occurred. As you reflect on the moment, imagine the outcome if you could have prevented it from happening or had the ability to recognize the "shady" behavior at the outset or even during the process. Picture in your mind's eye how things could have ended so differently. We often use the phrase "Hindsight is 20/20," but what about the foresight right in front of you? Shouldn't that vision be even clearer when it's right in your face? What causes us to be so blind in some areas that catch and hold our interest but so alert, focused, and vigilant in matters regarding those we love or things we feel cautious or overprotective about? Are we as individuals overly naive or too trusting of others based on what they tell us during our interactions?

In this book, I will share how to read and understand the universal facial expressions we all exhibit as well as some key areas of the body and movements that highlight comfort, stress, and other behaviors and emotions. While there are a ton of body language gestures and cues, this book will touch on some of the basic displays you may be exposed to on a daily basis.

As a law enforcement officer with over two decades of patrol and investigative experience, I am fortunate to have been exposed to a myriad of individuals from all walks of life. The opportunity to investigate incidents and crimes such as barking dogs, loud noise complaints, motor vehicle accidents, fraud, and homicides have put me face-to-face with many people. I've interacted with people during some of their best times as well as during the worst times of their lives.

This exposure has opened my eyes to things that many people will never see and can only imagine. As a rookie officer, I was not as well versed in reading and understanding body language as I thought. I was very trusting in believing what I heard but not always what I saw. However, once adequately seasoned, I received additional training as a polygraph examiner and attended some unique courses to enhance my skills. I have also received continuation training in interviewing and interrogation, micro expressions, body language, the art of elicitation, Chinese face reading, Reiki (energy work), and hypnosis. In addition, I've been afforded the opportunity to become certified as an instructor in many areas that have allowed me to share this information with other law enforcement officers and those outside of the law enforcement community interested in learning more about human behavior and analyzing traits involving truth and deception.

Because of the training and daily interactions my career has exposed me to, I've had an opportunity to help many people through tough times in their personal and professional lives. Understanding human behavior and distinguishing facts from fiction while analyzing the congruency of the words one speaks with what their body is saying is especially powerful. Training others and having them share their experiences of seeing things they had previously never paid attention to is one of the best rewards an instructor could receive. Based on my interactions with law enforcement officers, medical community members, human resource managers, social workers, energy work practitioners, and aspiring entrepreneurs, I contend that any professional interacting with people can benefit from the materials presented in this book and use the information immediately.

Through my law enforcement training, I have experience in working with victims, suspects, witnesses, applicants, etc., and I have been able to better recognize traits and behaviors within myself that allow me to build rapport with others. With the proper understanding and use of the information you learn in this book, your skill in interacting with others will give you a strategic and tactical advantage in areas where others fail.

I am happy to share what I have learned with the hope and expectation that people will be better able to understand one another to improve their communication efforts.

If you want to learn more about yourself while also learning about others, this book will be useful in getting you results. *I Can See What Your Body Is Saying* represents what is right before our eyes—seeing beyond purposeful distractions. The foundation of learning how to read others can start at any time and on any level. In your quest to discover more about body language and micro expression behaviors by diving into this book, you will expand your current knowledge and arm yourself with information that will strengthen your ability to truly understand what others are saying to you, even when they are not speaking out loud.

Chapter Two

WHEN THERE IS A LACK OF SKILL

Without Knowledge, Skill cannot be focused. Without Skill, Strength cannot be brought to bear and without Strength, Knowledge may not be applied.

~ ALEXANDER THE GREAT

I had been duped. While patrolling as a young officer, I conducted what many would consider a routine traffic stop. I pulled a vehicle over for speeding, and the person I stopped did not have any identification with him. The driver appeared to be a bit nervous, but I attributed it to the infrequency of his being stopped by the police and forgetting his wallet at home. I collected his name, date of birth, address, and other pertinent information and returned to my patrol car, verified the information was correct, and wrote the appropriate charge on a citation for the traffic violation. As I returned to his vehicle, the driver watched me wide-eyed in his driver-side mirror. Once the citation was issued, the thankful and apologetic driver drove away.

About two weeks later, I was working my beat and received a notification to report to the front desk; someone was there who wished to speak with me. I met the gentleman in the lobby of the police department, and he introduced himself. I thought the name sounded familiar as he provided me with his driver's license. He explained that he had received several letters in the mail from attorneys willing to represent him for his upcoming court date, a court date for which I had written a ticket in his name. I told him I did not recognize him, and he replied that it was because we had never met, but I had met his brother. He described his brother in detail and explained he had recently been using his name and information to get out of traffic tickets. He also gave me his brother's actual name and information and indicated he had warrants for his arrest, which was why he was using a false name. I had this individual wait while I checked his brother's information. The information was valid. I apologized for the error and the inconvenience he had suffered and explained I would contact the appropriate officials to correct this mishap.

Once he was gone, I realized I had been duped. All of the small nuances from that traffic stop started to come to mind. The over-politeness, the wide eyes during the reapproach . . . I had overlooked gestures and cues that day. Hindsight for me was 20/20 as my vision cleared. My eyes were opened to some areas I had been blinded in due to my inability to recognize this individual's deceptive behavior. I learned some valuable lessons that day that I carried with me throughout my career. With that new mindset, I was on my way to search the city for my suspect, who I later found and charged appropriately.

Proficiency in the craft is paramount to being highly regarded and qualified to perform certain professions. Even experts once started as newbies and eventually perfected their trade. As a practitioner of micro expressions and body language, I know the struggles and fears I had to overcome in gaining this expertise.

Throughout my career, I have observed officers (young and old) who professed to have specific skills in interviewing and interrogation but were not always capable of recognizing traits of deception when put in situations that demanded this skill. As I began to learn, I recognized my past failures and did everything possible to prevent them from recurring. Through speaking with novices and well-versed individuals on many aspects of nonverbal and verbal communication, I have realized that the difficulty in achieving higher levels of learning comes from a lack of specific knowledge involving looking and listening, or SKILL.

SKILL stands for **S**pecific **K**nowledge **I**nvolving **L**ooking and **L**istening.

Specific—the "what is it that I am looking for; what is being sought out" when communicating with another.

One needs to know precisely or unquestionably what they are seeking, or they may overlook what is directly in front of them. Being specific provides guidance and direction and prevents one from becoming sidetracked or derailed during a conversation. As an interviewer, are you looking for names of people or businesses, or perhaps dates and times? It is so easy to get sidetracked in a conversation when focus is not a priority or when dealing with someone who is great at avoiding hot topics. You may start talking about credit cards, and before you know it, the conversation has shifted to their child's soccer practice. I call these individuals escape artists, as they are great at getting away from things that would normally hold them down and keep them locked in place. When searching for specifics, one must know how to direct their questions and determine how and when to use open-ended questions to acquire information as well as closed-ended questions to clarify previous statements. Questions without a purpose may lead nowhere and cause you to end up with useless information if you don't have a game plan. Staying on track and controlling your conversation will prevent wasted time and get you the information you need in a timely manner.

Knowledge—the "what is and what is not" in a conversation.

Knowledge in itself is the facts or information on a subject. You can never have too much knowledge. What you decide to share and how you use it is entirely up to you. If talking about sailboats and you are well versed in sailing, this can be to your benefit when you hear something that contradicts what you know to be fact. When analyzing or searching for traits of truth and deception, the mastery of knowing what micro expressions are as well as their meaning in conjunction with body language is essential. Many people fail in the knowledge category because their library of actual knowledge about the topic and what to look for and exclude is minimal and limited. Studies have shown that during professional exchanges of information, many people do not truly understand the potential of nonverbal signals, nor are they able to accurately interpret facial signals and their meanings when needed.

Involving—the "surrounding, engaging, or association of something" in a situation.

Being involved shows engagement and links two or more people together during communication. There should be a direct state of *inclusion* rather than *exclusion* that demonstrates active participation to ensure the speaker is engaged with the listener and the listener is linked with the speaker. Just as this letter is located in the center of the acronym, it is central to the concept. If one or more parties are not involved when communicating with another, and the other party recognizes this, rapport can be lost and the chain can be broken. Once broken, it may be impossible to put back together to produce the desired outcome, and the remaining skills may be useless at that point. Involvement requires patience. Patience is a must when interacting with individuals in negotiating business transactions, acquiring information, and even in interviewing processes. Each person has their own way of speaking and trying to get their point across, and some take longer than others. Because of this, frustration can come easily and create interference within conversations. Being involved shows one is committed—not looking at their cell phone or paying attention to the time on their watch. No person ever wants to feel as if they are being ignored when speaking to someone, as it may come across as disrespectful.

Looking—the "ability to see" what is being demonstrated or shown.

As one has the opportunity to see things for what they really are, their vision is enhanced. When viewing things in the dark, our thought process can be distorted, and we may have or provide inaccurate details. In the dark, we may see things that appear to have moved but were actually still, or we may create something in our mind's eye that does not actually exist. However, when light (enlightenment) is introduced, we are able to see things with greater clarity. Can you remember a time when you were awake in the middle of the night and saw something on a chair or dresser in your room that appeared to be something completely different from what it actually was? I can recall times in my life, especially as a child, when I woke up and thought I saw a monster staring at me in the chair across from my bed. I would lay there petrified and afraid to move, but as I began to focus my eyes, or if any form of light became available as cars passed or the sun came up, it was easier to notice that it was just a stuffed animal or a pile of clothes that had appeared to be something completely different. Even in the dark (or when metaphorically lost), one can train their eyes to see fact from fiction; it merely takes practice. As a firearms instructor, I have noticed that the majority of officers I have trained and qualified tend to shoot better at night than during the day. Their shot groupings are a lot tighter, and their scores typically increase. Why is that? During daytime shooting, distractions often occur; officers are looking at other officers' targets, and many of them feel rather confident when they can see they are doing well without having to wonder whether they are passing. However, at night, when significantly less light is available, the need to focus on what's directly in front of them demands every bit of their attention.

Listening—the "ability to hear and take notice" of what one is saying.

To hear is not a difficult task. It is simply the ability to recognize and perceive sounds, whether in the background, in the distance, or right in front of you. However, taking notice of what is heard requires attention and focus. When listening, one must actively be alert to hear what is being expressed, think about and process what was heard, and decide what to do with the information received. Even though both hearing and listening involve the use of ears, they are not the same. In communication, this is essential in conjunction with the other parts of the SKILL acronym. With listening, the ability to recognize specific words and phrases as part of analyzing an individual's statements is also vital. The words we use in conversation, especially during intense or high-stakes moments, are usually chosen to relay the message that we want heard as opposed to what may have truly happened.

By knowing which areas of **SKILL** one is lacking, they can target any area they feel they need to improve or strengthen.

A person could read numerous books and watch movies on various subjects, but does that classify them as an expert for that material? For that matter, are they even able to claim to be a practitioner? For any information to be effective, we must put it into practice. Unfortunately, depending on their profession or daily activities, some may not have many opportunities to perform the skills they have read about or seen. For example, reading books on chemistry does not make one a chemist, studying the history and operations of the Federal Bureau of Investigation (FBI) does not make one an FBI agent, and watching videos on music production does not make one a producer.

Studies have been developed in recent years and decades to determine people's accuracy in determining truth-lie judgments. In other words, how good is someone at detecting whether another is telling the truth or lying based on what is presented before them? A study done in 2006 by Bond and DePaulo indicated that individuals had an accuracy rate of 54 percent in detecting deception. That accuracy rate is nearly comparable to doing a coin toss and calling heads or tails, which is obviously problematic when attempting to determine someone's innocence or guilt.

Research has also shown that many individuals are more truth-biased when interpreting truth and deception in others. This means that we as individuals tend to judge messages presented to us as truthful rather than deceitful. This would especially be the case when interacting with people we know and are familiar with in our daily lives. After all, if we were to walk around all day believing that everything communicated to us is a lie, when and why would we ever trust or believe in anyone? As humans, we naturally tend to believe those we know unless we are given information that causes us to believe otherwise.

In the judicial system, expert witnesses are often called to the stand during court proceedings to provide information to validate the evidence. When jury members are involved, they make their decision by evaluating the information presented to them to determine proof beyond a reasonable doubt.

Experts are sought because they have extensive knowledge, training, and experience in the field, and they are far better versed than others in a specific subject, which classifies them as subject matter experts or SMEs.

As you begin your journey by reading this book, you will have created an opportunity to build a foundation to further enhance any thoughts or concepts in the study of nonverbal communication. While everyone learns at a different pace, I encourage you to keep an open mind, as the information contained here is well within your reach. As the saying goes, "Rome wasn't built in a day," so the expectation to learn and use this information within days, weeks, months, or years depends on you. There is no right or wrong amount of time to supplement and improve your education.

There are several reasons or excuses people give when claiming to be unable to learn a new skill or trait. Fortunately for all, there are not too many things within that can hinder one's ability to learn body language and micro expressions or the energetic connections that individuals display when relaxed or stressed. Whether one is a teenager or in their sixties or seventies, age is not an issue. Because we all have learned to recognize traits and characteristics of behavior from birth—and our ability to see, hear, talk, and communicate in some form or fashion has been used throughout our lives—some of the information in this book may be things you already know, with other information building on it or being completely new or now more relevant to you in your life.

Considerations of time to study and how long before results can be achieved may also create obstacles to one's desire to learn. Quitting is easy as it takes little to no effort; however, overcoming obstacles is possible with planning and desire. We all make time for important things in our lives. When learning, remember that we place the boundaries and limitations on ourselves based on our internal belief system. We learn new things each day, whether consciously or unconsciously. When we take a moment and look around, we can see people from all walks of life earn their General Educational Development diplomas (GEDs), high school diplomas, and associate's, bachelor's, master's, and doctorate degrees at different ages for a variety of reasons.

The ability to awaken one's inner skills and abilities is far greater than we can imagine. The power contained within the mind, once open, will reveal things that have always been right in front of us but sometimes hidden in plain sight. The benefit of having things revealed and being shown how to continue the path of learning should be never-ending.

Obstacles are merely temporary hindrances designed to slow down one's work in progress. As you have already tapped into your inner self to venture down this path, understanding these nonverbal methods of communication will get easier once you develop a sound foundation and learn the principles.

As you continue reading, the development phases of understanding nonverbal communication will be implemented, and you will have a greater ability to utilize your newfound skills, which will begin to make themselves visible to you with little to no delay.

Chapter Three
THE ROAD MAP
TO SUCCESS

**All you need is the plan, the road map, and
the courage to press on to your destination.**
~ EARL NIGHTINGALE

W hen I transitioned departments from being a traffic enforcement officer to investigating criminal cases and regulating businesses, I did not have any formal experience in interviewing. As stated earlier, I suffered from a lack of **SKILL**, so frustration sometimes presented itself during my daily activities. In many investigations, I was very fortunate to have direct evidence that was undeniable, and my suspects would usually confess with little to no interrogation. I had received basic instruction in the police academy on how to complete reports and acquired field experience in speaking with people, but I had not been properly trained on conducting criminal interviews. My experience level was that of a novice as my only knowledge of how to do interviews was based on watching television shows about detectives and listening to a handful of tips from my peers. Basically, I was clueless.

Once I started getting assigned cases where I needed to dig deep or met with resistance in gathering information, I didn't know what to do as it was unfamiliar territory for me. Unfortunately, you don't know what you don't know. I couldn't stop in the middle of an interview and go find someone to take over for me, as I felt that would make me seem incompetent to both the suspect and my coworkers. I requested to attend additional classes for training and was often turned down due to our being short-staffed. I remember building up vacation leave to attend an interview and interrogation school that I saw advertised at a local community college and had to have. It was a forty-hour block of instruction that took place over one week. The best part about this class was it was free of charge. All I had to do was register, show up, and take the training.

I remember meeting the instructor on the first day. He was a retired FBI agent who worked back in the '70s and '80s. This gray-haired, seasoned gentleman was excited about teaching us what he knew. The information I learned in that one week was unbelievable. He shared some great stories with us about people he had investigated during his career. I learned about key phrases to look for and techniques to use that I wished I had known before. I watched videos and shook my head in disappointment as I said to myself, "I had the same situation happen to me just weeks ago." Interestingly, many students in the class were in the same predicament that I was, with a very low knowledge base in interviewing and interrogating. However, at the end of the week, I felt much more confident with the information I had received, and I was prepared to take on new challenges.

I was back in the field interviewing suspects, witnesses, and victims on a regular basis and sat in one day on a suspect interview with a coworker that had a few more years of experience. This particular case was interesting as it involved notary fraud. The suspect was alleged to have been notarizing motor vehicle sale documents without the presence of the required parties in front of him. The person he was doing the notarizations for was involved in several criminal transactions regarding illegal vehicle title transfers.

During this particular interview, the suspect was at a point of resistance and did not want to budge even though his notary seal and signature were present on several fraudulent documents. I switched interviewing roles with my coworker and began to ask our suspect some questions relating to the transactions. Fortunately, we got a break. I noticed the suspect had a moment of thought and began to consider the consequences while also realizing that all other options had been exhausted. During his moment of silence, he leaned forward and put his head down, looking at the floor as he rested his forearms on his thighs. His hands were gently clasped, and I noticed how he lightly rubbed one of his thumbs across the back of the other as if to console himself. His mouth gesture showed an inward pull of both lips and a brief frown. I allowed the moment of silence to provide him with the opportunity to have some internal conversation and reflection to do the right thing and admit to his wrongdoing. Suddenly, a deep inhale was followed by a long exhale as though there were some relief and he was about to lift this weight from his shoulders. As he completed his sigh, my coworker, in a demanding tone, asked something to the effect of "Are you going to sit there all day, or are you going to say something?" Once the suspect raised his head back up, I immediately knew our connection had been broken and all efforts to obtain a confession were lost. His facial expression went from sadness to anger and frustration. He looked at both of us and said he would like to leave and speak with an attorney, and our meeting was done.

I asked myself what had just happened, as I was shocked and could not believe it. How did my coworker not see what I saw? Was he not trained and well versed, or was he tired and frustrated from the time spent interviewing the suspect? I then realized that all levels and skill sets were not equal, and everyone had different abilities to connect with people. As we spoke about the circumstances after the suspect's departure, my coworker felt that he would not have provided any information and his silence was just a stalling technique. I explained my theory of the suspect's actions based on what I had learned, but we agreed to disagree. Unfortunately, due to the suspect leaving and hiring an attorney, neither of us would ever know for certain.

Visual obstacles can be imagined or theorized as large or small as you make them. In other words, not all roadblocks are permanent and impassable, and not all mountains are unclimbable. At times, we may feel that some of the challenges we face in communicating with others are impossible to overcome, but this is far from the truth. There is usually a way to get around every obstacle; however, some take more time than others as one may have to approach the situation from different angles and points of view to test their theory.

Even though we may have been scammed or lied to in the past, this does not mean that trend will continue until the end of time. Luckily, resources such as this book are available for us to train and learn the valuable skills that can help protect us and others from being victims of circumstance. In your pursuit of seeing what the body is saying, your ability to learn and apply the information within will become easier as the days progress. Every problem is only temporary as nothing lasts forever. That being said, know that solutions to feeling uncomfortable or lacking confidence in recognizing truthful, deceptive, and noncongruent behavior are within reach.

Discovering solutions is metaphorically like finding and reading a map to a treasure chest. Some may consider it to be like a scavenger hunt. The clues are provided. One merely must decipher the information, and voilà, gold at last!

Throughout my life, let alone my career, I have always been a seeker of knowledge. In that pursuit, I have encountered many obstacles that hindered my desire to learn the art of reading and understanding others. I have spent a lot of time studying useful and useless information and contributing funds toward grasping the knowledge I now possess. Because of these headaches, I wanted to create a guide or path to show others in a brief but informative manner what I have learned in law enforcement over the past twenty years. In that effort, the information presented throughout this book will help you overcome many obstacles you may encounter by creating a path of knowledge and enlightenment.

Understanding Energy and the Body as One

Since we as humans are innately energetic, the ability to see energy shifts and changes within others is quite simple when we understand what we see. The energy within an individual can be positive as well as negative. Have you ever been in a room where things seem cheerful and positive, and then someone enters, and in the blink of an eye everyone gets quiet and the mood changes? Or maybe the situation was the exact opposite: you had been depressed or "down in the dumps," and then someone came around and immediately brightened your day. This is an example of how energy can interrupt specific patterns and behavior when conversing with or observing others.

When we can recognize which areas of the body are affected energetically, we have a better idea of how to interact with others in specific situations. Observing energy shifts within an individual provides us with an understanding of when there are blockages and clearances. Being armed with the ability to see these nuances allows one to understand the emotional states of an individual at the moment they are displayed. These blockages are expressed through movements and gestures recognized as body language, but they energetically allow us to understand what part of an individual is being affected within their body.

Body Language Basics

As the mind speaks to a person, so does the body.

Even when an individual's lips are sealed, under the right circumstances, the body reveals information about the truth of what's going on behind the scenes in the brain. We have three parts of the brain that are responsible for our behavior and actions. These are the reptilian, mammalian, and neocortex. The reptilian brain consists of the brain stem and the cerebellum, which assists us with our balance and equilibrium, as well as our survival instincts, breathing, heart rate, and body temperature. The mammalian or limbic brain records memories and houses our emotions. Finally, the neocortex has been identified as the newest part of the brain, hence its prefix "neo." It provides us with the abilities of logic, reasoning, and speaking and learning other languages, as well as enabling us to have conscious thought over the decisions we make. The roles they play instinctively keep us protected in times of stress as well as relaxation. It is primarily because of these parts of the brain that we have survived positive and negative experiences in our lifetime.

Our natural ability to interpret body language can be interrupted through words that are spoken to us. Fortunately, to our benefit, the mind constantly remains alert to scan for errors and details to interpret discrepancies. This mental detector acts on our behalf as the facilitator to recognize when things seem incongruent. In comparison to the language being spoken, an individual's body language should flow smoothly and be consistent with what is being said. One's body parts (limbs) can have many different functions and abilities, and so can the meanings they demonstrate outwardly to others.

Reading Facial Expressions—Micro Expression Basics

Observing facial expressions has been a key part of our lives since birth. You have been reading facial expressions to understand others all your life, whether you realize it or not. It's important to recognize that the face is full of information and is one of the key areas we focus on during our interactions with others. Before we even learned to speak our native or secondary languages, we were communicating with every part of our face as the various parts (mouth, nose, eyes, eyebrows, cheeks, forehead, and lips) worked in tandem with each other.

Because of this, the ability to see what one's body is saying is not something new, and the face comprises items and functions that we may have temporarily set aside and just need a refresher on what they do and how they operate. The task of learning and understanding these expressions is not complicated as it is inherently within us to be able to do this. Even while wearing masks during the COVID-19 pandemic, we learned to modify our scope of vision and somewhat shifted our focus to the eyes to seek information, as well as watching for the rising and falling of the mask when we felt that others might be smiling or frowning. As stated earlier, the information is already programmed inside of you, and this book is going to give you a reboot to see things in a different light as the face can be seen in zones, in sections, or in its entirety.

Understanding Combinations

Because one movement does not always signify one exact thing per se, it is important to know that information received from the mouth, face, and body must sometimes be evaluated in combinations. In other words, do the words being spoken match the movements of the face? The motion of a foot tapping up and down that makes it appear that one is nervous could potentially be due to the conversation being held, or could it be that the person has anxiety issues, and that is how they relax? It is critical to have a great deal of information formed from a baseline before formulating a conclusion on what to believe.

Understanding combinations is much like understanding what happens when different colors are blended. When yellow and blue are mixed, they create the color green. When one draws in their lips tightly, inhales deeply, and crosses their arms across their chest, anger and frustration are in the air. However, when one of these actions is done independently, it alone doesn't constitute anger or frustration even though it may be an ingredient of that recipe. Learning to recognize these combinations (or their absence) in comparison to verbal statements will help you see where there may be a lack of congruency that requires further examination. As you are introduced to these areas of the body and how they correlate to specific emotions, actions, and behaviors in the subsequent chapters, your understanding of how combinations reveal themselves will truly blossom.

How to See What the Body Is Saying

The ability to take the things we have learned in life and apply them in some form or fashion only makes sense. At times during our lives, we may learn things at different intervals and never really have the opportunity to utilize the information. For some, it may seem like useless knowledge. However, any information acquired, depending on what the individual desires to do with it, creates an opportunity for continued learning. Learning a new skill is truly beneficial, but putting it to use reveals one's level of proficiency.

Reading the information shared in this book will provide you with a knowledge base to understand what signs of information are demonstrated before you and others. Actively interacting with and observing others in the real world will allow you to explore what you have learned by noticing actions and reactions in their true form more clearly.

In learning to read others and understand what is being said nonverbally, a great deal of information is provided to us with and without conversation. The easy part of understanding the information contained in this book has already been in place since your creation and birth. The only challenge you may face is not truly putting all the knowledge provided to you into daily practice to gain a higher level of expertise. While you may not want to ultimately become recognized as an expert, putting the information in the next few chapters into action will be useful as you encounter unique, odd, or even everyday life situations with others.

We have only scratched the surface of what you will understand when your eyes are truly opened to what is in front of you. As an example, I would like to share an encouraging story from a former student in some of my training who works in the dental industry. My student had just finished assisting with an initial examination, where it was determined that the client needed some extensive work that would be a bit costly for someone without insurance. When the client was told the diagnosis and the necessary cost of treatment, my student initially observed signs of fear in his eyes, followed by sadness on the forehead and lips as the client attempted to conceal his emotion. Since the expressions were momentary, the person providing the information to the client did not see or interpret these emotions.

While the client attempted to reassure the dental assistant (my student) that all was fine and the cost would not be an issue, my student asked to speak to the finance department manager privately. A request was made to see what payment options were available so the client would not have to make one huge payment, allowing him to receive the much-needed procedure. An agreement was made and presented to the client as an option to assist him. Immediately, the client showed surprise on his forehead and happiness in his smile, in conjunction with a sigh of relief. The client began to open up and speak freely about some financial issues he was going through and acknowledged he was appreciative of the options. Interestingly, at the onset of the situation, he had been closed up and did not want to convey much information due to fear. As a result of the dental assistant seeing and understanding what was going on behind the scenes and what emotions were felt at the time, the situation was addressed without delay, resulting in the retention of a client who later referred others to the practice based on its willingness to assist him with his financial concerns.

How amazing it is to know that seeing and understanding how to address emotional situations without delay can produce long-term benefits for many in the end!

Chapter Four

THE MECHANICS OF READING OTHERS

He that has eyes to see and ears to hear
may convince himself that no mortal
can keep a secret. If his lips are silent,
he chatters with his fingertips; betrayal
oozes out of him at every pore.
~ SIGMUND FREUD

From the day we are born and begin to use our eyes, we learn to recognize facial expressions. Within parent-to-child and child-to-parent interactions, there is an exchange of expressions and behavior that we learn to understand. It has been hardwired into our DNA. We see our parents smile and make facial expressions in an effort to get us to smile. We see the gestures they make to get us to laugh, and we learn rather quickly how to get their attention even though we aren't able to speak. We learn our parents' faces when they are happy, sad, frustrated, angry, and so on, and we can often see children begin to imitate certain movements and gestures.

Once a child begins to learn how to speak, what happens? Monitoring and observation seem to become less necessary as we now have learned a new language called verbal communication. More often than not, we tend to believe the words we hear from others as opposed to what we originally knew as our primary form of communication. But we still have bits and pieces of it as we are now learning congruency—with spoken words, body language, and the facial expressions we first learned.

As a child begins to get older, tantrums are not allowed and corrective behavior is taught. Children are expected to behave in a manner that conforms with societal norms, so they begin to learn how to suppress or better control their temper in hard situations. We reinforce certain behaviors when difficult times are in front of them . . . keep your head up; it will be OK. Stand up straight . . . stop slouching. We see that when people are victorious in competitive events, they put their hands up, while the loser keeps their hands down.

As these expressions are presented, in conjunction with what is being said, we learn to understand the behavior of others and ultimately recognize what is expected to accompany this behavior as it is being demonstrated. For example, can you remember a time as a child you did something that upset your parents or teacher? Can you visualize the gestures they made in addition to what they said? A parent's verbal statement to their child to "Get over here and sit down right now or else" can create an immediate reaction of compliance based on how it was demonstrated and voiced.

Tone of voice, facial expression, and hand gestures will work in tandem with the statement to communicate this demand. Also, in some circumstances, a parent may be in an environment where they can't verbalize their demand, so they display facial expressions (anger) and body language gestures (finger-pointing) to get their point across to their child.

Most of us probably saw these facial expressions and body language gestures as children while in a grocery or department store when we were either asking for something we knew we could not have or doing something we knew we were not supposed to be doing. More often than not, children know and understand these signs and immediately correct the actions to avoid any consequences at a later time.

As we are not born with genuine concern or knowledge of fear, we are willing to take chances as toddlers. However, as we get older and realize that things in life are not always favorable, we tend to become hesitant, which keeps us from moving forward. As a result, many will never pursue their dreams or will be afraid to even try for fear of failure.

Generally, as a part of human nature, we tend to believe what we see in front of us. After all, most of us have heard and lived by the statement "seeing is believing." Even during magic shows or feats of illusion, a part of us wants to believe that what the magician is doing is real, even though we know many feats they perform are not humanly possible.

Most people are dazzled in disbelief and cannot believe what they see, and they will usually ask the magician to "Do it again!" to see if they can spot what is fact from fiction. In body language and micro expressions, what we see may very well be real or fake in presentation. As we see behaviors or changes, we need to believe what we observe and ultimately determine its authenticity. As a body language interpreter or analyst, one must learn to recognize baseline behavior and quickly interpret and understand the individual being observed and their "norms." This observation of baseline behavior and shifts is vital in understanding others. It is similar to listening to music and noticing patterns in the drum track or the addition or deletion of instruments in the background. Every item has a role, and its presence or absence can make a huge difference in maintaining focus or losing interest.

As a polygraph examiner, I was taught to believe in my polygraph charts. These charts were the information that was printed out from the physiological recordings that took place during the polygraph examination. As a new examiner, I had to quickly realize that what was displayed on my computer monitor or printouts was very much real. While the polygraph instrument aided in measuring and recording physiological changes within the body, a person's outward appearance could seem undisturbed or without change.

It did not take long before I understood that the polygraph was not an actual lie detector as I had heard many people call it in the past. It did not indicate whether a person was telling the truth or being deceptive, but it recorded various responses from an individual's body and their specific movements as they responded to a stimulus—in other words, the questions I was asking. As equipment that aids in capturing respiration rates, sweat gland activity (electrodermal response) on the fingertips, blood pressure variances, and pulse rates, this instrument is an awesome tool in its functionality and capabilities.

During pretest interviews, polygraph examiners question their interviewees to obtain information that later assists them in the formulation of questions to ask on the polygraph test. This is a vital step in the process, as with any form of talking to, interviewing, or questioning an individual; if you are not asking the "right" questions, then you will not collect the "right" response. Interestingly, it was amazing to see how calm a person could appear on the outside while answering questions verbally, but when later connected to the polygraph instrument, it became evident that several internal physiological reactions were taking place in their body. How could this be? How could a person seem so calm and answer a question with a straight face, seemingly unbothered, but later appear as though they were having an anxiety or panic attack inside their body?

Recognizing nervousness, anxiety, anger, fear, and other emotions can eventually become easier as the eye is trained to look for the small nuances and movements that take place when these emotions occur. The autonomic nervous system is the controller of what happens when the body experiences sympathetic nervous system responses to situations involving fight, flight, or freezing.

As the sympathetic nervous system is engaged, the physiological reactions of fight, flight, or freezing are uncontrollable by an individual. They will occur when the body feels threatened, stressed, or nervous and assist when an individual needs to protect themself from danger or harm. The body will produce more sweat and blood pressure will increase. The pupils will dilate to ensure focus, muscles will expand to allow more blood flow, and the digestive system will restrict bowel movements.

Once the threat is lessened, the parasympathetic nervous system assists in bringing the body back to a relaxed or normal state. This can be described as that feeling of being on a roller-coaster ride. Once it starts to approach the top, the sympathetic nervous system prepares the body for what it knows is coming next—the downhill rush, twists, turns, and loops. The heart begins to beat faster, some individuals grip the support bars tighter, and the body takes action to keep itself safe. However, once the ride is over and the roller coaster comes to rest, the body realizes that it is now safe and begins to relax as the threat of danger and fear subside. At this point, you will often see people start to relax, loosen up, laugh, and talk about their experiences.

I asked the question earlier how someone could seem so calm on the outside but physiologically show anxiety or panic on the inside when taking the polygraph. As the examinee is connected to the various items of equipment, they are told at the beginning of the test to remain as still as possible. They are seated in a chair with their feet flat on the floor and their arms adjacent to the sides of their body. This position does not allow for movement during the test as it could create interference or distortion in their chart recordings. However, when the body senses a threat or has an emotional response to a situation, thought, or circumstance, it wants to take action to protect itself. While connected to the polygraph instrument, one is restricted from movement such as tapping the feet or rubbing the fingers or any other self-soothing mannerisms, and therefore the body adjusts to the circumstance as best as it can. As a result, the instrument records which areas of the body are being affected based on their response either during the asking of the question or within seconds after answering.

The individual taking the polygraph does not beat the *polygraph*. They beat the *examiner*. In other words, some can manipulate and convince the examiner that the results are inaccurate regardless of what was recorded during their examination. The polygraph instrument is merely a tool that may aid in confirming suspicions based on earlier observations during pretest interviewing.

Some people are so good at convincing others that even when we know or strongly suspect they are lying to us, we tend to believe them. Hence, the term "con man." These individuals are extremely *confident* in their practice of gaining others' trust, and they appear to be genuine and honest, which causes many to lower their guard. This theory translated into a new mindset that taught me to be aware and cognizant of what I saw displayed on my charts despite what I may have heard. After all, the reactions I saw on the polygraph charts were produced by the interviewee's bodily responses, not the words they spoke. However, it was my job to delve deeper based on the totality of the circumstances to make an educated determination of what to do next and if I should question further on specific areas. It was also my job to determine whether the recordings on the chart were congruent with the nonverbal indicators that I received or did not receive during my initial conversation and interview process.

In learning to develop the skill of recognizing body language and micro expressions, one should not be afraid to be incorrect. Being wrong, along with drive, motivation, and resiliency, helps one become better at being correct. If or when a "gut feeling" is perceived, use the skills you have learned to hone in on the issue. Through additional questioning, one can eventually come to an informed conclusion about their theories.

As human beings, whether we are intentionally trying to be deceptive, overexaggerating a story, or even being polite when we do not want to be, we want to make sure that others believe what we are saying, doing, or both. In other words, we must ensure that others will buy what we are selling to them. If we are not convincing enough, we fear that they will see through our cover stories and recognize that we are being untruthful.

Let's face it, anyone with something to hide when confronted about an uncomfortable topic has probably already rehearsed their story. Many will play the "well if" game: "Well, if they ask me this, I will say that," or "Well, if they ask me that, I will say this." In a nutshell, they have enough confidence in themselves to believe that whatever questions are asked of them, their answers will be satisfactory enough to prevent further probing.

As a body language analyzer and decoder, before stepping in the ring with the bull, be prepared and believe that you will be able to recognize anything that appears outside the norm. If you are hesitant and nervous, those feelings will often manifest themselves and show up in the faces of others.

As stated earlier, children learn to recognize their parents' faces and behavioral signs during their infancy and toddler stages of life. Because parents know this, they create funny faces and actions. They believe they will successfully cause their child to laugh at them; otherwise, they would not perform the action.

If one specific facial expression does not work, they try something different until they achieve the desired outcome. The same theory and principle apply to those trying to deceive. If one story fails, their mindset is "I'll modify it until it works or is believable." Once it works, the thought is to continue using the story until it is time to change it to something new. After all, why would someone change a story that has worked well for them? Trying to make it better or omitting information creates a need to remember new or more information and can create hiccups during transmission. Because of this, it is vital to take mental note of what is being displayed when the emotions and reactions show themselves. More importantly, good interviewers, salespeople, and conversationalists are aware and expect that specific expressions may be displayed based on the questions they have preplanned or are preparing to ask an individual when searching for information.

Being a body language practitioner means being prepared to change your methods of seeking and gaining information to get the outcome you want. This will also help you to be able to adjust and overcome difficult situations when working with different individuals and personalities. Remember, there is not just one tactic that fits all situations and scenarios.

Just as I was taught to believe what I read in my charts, trust and believe that you will be able to read an individual's body language as you converse with them. Asking stimulating or provocative questions and observing the individual's behavior before, during, and after answering will allow you to understand what is occurring behind the scenes. Their actions will be the lines and information written on the charts. Every detail of information provided to you will assist in giving you an entire reading of the individual.

As an important part of the process, be mindful and understand that not everyone is going to respond equally or show reactions in a manner that you may expect. Because we all come from different cultures, ethnicities, life experiences, and backgrounds, we must be open to the fact that not everyone will react as we think they will. Depending on an individual's values, beliefs, moral compass, attitudes, and experiences in life, their reactions will vary. A person's values are what they have acquired and hold dear as being useful or important based on their societal patterns or socialization, while their beliefs are what they hold to be true or accept in their life. Their attitudes are based on how they feel about things and are displayed in their actions, while their experiences are the events that have taken place throughout their life that have molded the character that stands before you. In other words, just because someone is not showing sadness in a situation in which you would normally feel sad does not mean that they are not sad. They may not grieve or display grief in the same manner as you. Not everyone will be angry or disgusted or fearful of situations that you think they should be because that's how "everyone else" would react. However, keep the observation in your memory as you build your database of information on who you are speaking with and learn who they are as an individual.

Confidence is built from trials and tribulations. It stems from the ability to believe in oneself. As we become more proficient in our craft, the feeling of comfort and relaxation is a bit more obvious, which shows in our performance. Belief in ourselves comes from a state of mind in which we feel that what we desire to do will be successful. No matter how much others may believe in your ability to do something, if you don't have an ounce of belief in yourself, you are unlikely to make it a reality.

Chapter Five

UNDERSTANDING ENERGY AND THE BODY

The feedback between mind and body is being replenished thousands of times a minute.
~ DEEPAK CHOPRA

Research has shown that understanding body language can create positive outcomes. Some studies have examined the role of nonverbal communication and educational performance between students and faculty, which has shown to have positive and profound effects. In business applications, nonverbal communication plays an important role in personnel evaluation, management and leadership aspects, emotions in the workplace, and sales and customer service. Unfortunately, research in some areas regarding business and organizational settings is scarce. However, in all aspects of business and leadership, the quality of communication between individuals and the relationships employees have with one another are always of interest and focus. In other areas, early recognition of specific signs can help defuse negative situations before they escalate to become dangerous. For example, throughout a law enforcement officer's career, a review of body camera footage and other video recordings reveals nonverbal indicators that assist in their training in verbal de-escalation tactics.

In other aspects of law enforcement, the understanding of specific nonverbal indicators aids in recognizing truthfulness and deception.

With everything we do as human beings involving movement and thought, there is a mind–body connection. When we think positive thoughts, our emotions tend to remain positive and upbeat and give us an overall sense of well-being and energetic balance. We usually feel comfortable or confident in our actions as our positivity is focused on good outcomes and behaviors as opposed to bad. On the other hand, when we have negative thoughts, we typically project a negative image toward others, and our well-being and feelings are usually disrupted as well. As a result of our inner struggles, we may feel stressed-out or display negative actions toward others who don't deserve them.

Just as food supplies the body as an energy source for nutrients to survive and function, the energy in our body language is expressed through our emotions and our mental, physical, and vocal actions. Some may call this the "vibe factor" as they are evaluating the vibration of energy in a positive or negative form, or they are sensing an emotional connection or disconnection from an individual. Energy is a source of liveliness and ultimately, a necessity for our survival. Because our brains and subconscious minds store all aspects of our past, we adapt and recognize behaviors and attitudes based on our previous experiences or exposures. When walking into a room or first meeting others, our brains process information so quickly that our senses assess what we see, hear, feel, touch, or taste immediately without our having to think about it. Without hesitation, we are evaluating others' moods and intentions based on how they are sitting or standing, facial cues, and body language.

It's interesting to see how we can read a person's energy in an instant when we pay attention to the information before us, which enables us to take action to protect ourselves. We often see similar behaviors or characteristics with animals and young children. There have been instances when pets are introduced to people and immediately, the animal shies away or growls as if to express dislike for that individual, when they are normally friendly and receptive to everyone. What is it about that person that the animal finds intrusive and does not want to be around? The same can also apply to babies and young children. Some children do not want to be around many people, but certain individuals when first introduced are intriguing or allowed to hold them and be in their space. In these situations, there is something about an individual's energetic aura or being that either draws or turns others away from being in their personal space.

As a continual seeker of knowledge, at one point during my studies I had the opportunity to learn about the **chakras of the body** and how they each relate to specific functions and organs in the body. For those unfamiliar with chakras, they are translated as wheels or a disk of spiritual energy flowing throughout the body along the spine. While these energetic disks are not physically visible to the naked eye, they are represented by unique colors with different meanings and influences specifically chosen to match that energy center. I was introduced to this information while taking a yoga class, which led me to learn about Reiki and its relationship to energy work. While multiple chakras and meridians throughout the body pertain to our energy and sense of well-being, we typically acknowledge and reference seven of them. These are the **root, sacral, solar plexus, heart, throat, third eye**, and **crown chakra**. While many of us typically observe others starting from the head on the basis of recognition, the basic structure of the chakras starts from the bottom and works its way up to the top; hence, "the root," as in roots of a tree, up to "the crown," which is on top of the head.

Interestingly, while these chakras have different locations on the body, I have been able to establish a correlation between people's energetic and emotional feelings during stressful situations and their body language and facial expressions. From those behaviors and actions, I am able to accurately measure congruency and authenticity of their true energetic or emotional state. I started noticing this correlation when speaking to people that had some type of emotional connection and response to what they were telling me about events. While I had been able to recognize specific gestures and movements and their meaning from previous training, a new outlook on the body in an energetic sense came into play for me. When chakra energy is low, blocked, or depleted, there is typically an inability or difficulty in expressing the particular qualities and traits associated with the area. In other words, a person may exhibit a lack of confidence, an inability to voice their opinions, and a lack of clarity, vision, or a sense of purpose in life. Having knowledge of what the chakras govern will give one an advantage in understanding what is happening internally on an energetic level with the mind–body connection, as it is done unintentionally. Ultimately, as there is no one gesture or cue for recognizing truth or deception, one should be mindful to look for patterns, changes, or shifts in behavior in conjunction with the movements of the face and body.

As you read over the next couple of pages, think about a time when you have either done these actions yourself or seen them in someone else to link what was being affected or how they were troubled based on what you know about the situation.

The **root chakra** is located by the base of the spine, including the legs, hips, and lower back, and relates to our sense of grounding, comfort, and security. It is our foundation for support and balance in relation to our survival. From the front, it is seen at or around and just below the groin area. It has an affirmation or catchphrase of "I am." As it correlates with the body and how it speaks to us, I've seen blockages or states of imbalance in how people will stand in front of others with their hands together while sometimes leaning or rocking side to side off-center, covering their groin area. This chakra is also involved in our fight-or-flight response triggers and may be displayed as fear, anxiety, or uncertainty. This can be seen from time to time when someone is put on the spot and has to speak in front of a crowd or is awaiting judgment or punishment before an authority figure (such as appearing before a judge or a parent scolding their child).

Quite often, there is a lack of eye contact. The head may be tilted downward, as though they are looking toward the floor with the chin lowered as opposed to high and prideful. If their head is not lowered, their eyes may frequently look down and away from what is in front of them. They may be pacing or fidgeting due to anxiety or be stiff and rigid as though in shock and unable to move as a result of fear or uncertainty. Suppose this is seen during a conversation (seated) after a touchy subject is mentioned or someone is placed in an uncomfortable predicament. In that case, one may also see the groin area being covered with the hands in between the legs to protect and give themselves a sense of security as they may be afraid and ungrounded. One may even see a leg begin to shake to release nervous energy, or if a leg was shaking and all of a sudden stops, a break or disruption has occurred. One may even cross their legs or stand in a way that appears unbalanced or unsteady. It is also not uncommon to see a person standing on both feet

but swaying their body from side to side as though rocking themselves subconsciously to alleviate nervous energy built up within their body.

I remember during some of my workout routines when I would jog around my neighborhood, I would see a deputy sheriff patrol vehicle enter the area around the same time each afternoon, but I never saw it exit. I assumed there was a new officer around the corner from my house, but I hadn't had the opportunity to meet them. One particular day, I happened to see the vehicle backing into a driveway as I rounded the corner. I slowed my pace and stopped in front of their yard as they exited the vehicle and walked toward their mailbox. The young female deputy appeared a bit startled as I approached her to introduce myself. I said that I too was an officer and lived around the corner, and I told her which house was mine. As I started to create small talk and inquired about how long she had been on the job, what her plans were on the department, and who we knew in common, I noticed she began to rock from side to side as she spoke to me. It became obvious that she had nervous feet. She told me that she had only been on solo patrol for a couple of months and was relatively new to law enforcement. This was her first professional job, and she was still trying to figure out if it was going to be a good career choice for her. If she stopped moving her feet from side to side, she would move her arms back and forth from her sides to the front of her body to open-hand clap while she spoke. At the time, I only saw that she was a bit nervous as she was under pressure with some of the questions I asked her, and she may have felt slightly intimidated. Now that I can reflect on what was happening energetically, I believe she had a blocked root chakra because she was neither secure nor comfortable in the situation of answering questions as a rookie deputy being caught off guard. The movement or pacing of her feet showed that she was not grounded in her answers because she was uncertain about some of her decisions and was still trying to figure things out internally. Her body wanted to leave the conversation, but in order to remain polite, she stayed and dealt with her energetic emotions as best as she could. After a couple of minutes of this, I remember changing the conversation to the houses in the neighborhood and how it was a great time to purchase since the interest rates were at an all-time low, and her nervousness seemed to cease almost instantly. She stopped the rocking back and forth and side to side and told me about how excited she was to purchase her home and some of the aspects of her home-buying adventure. Her legs became more stable, and her hands and arms became more illustrative as she spoke about how she had found this neighborhood and how close it was to the department. I reflect back now on how one topic or shift in conversation can easily change one's blockages and flows within the body as the mind–body connection adjusts in an instant.

Because the root chakra relates to grounding and comfort, observe what takes place in this specific area involving the base of the spine and downward to the feet, which are our grounding platform. It is very possible to see another area being affected as well in conjunction with this chakra. Be mindful and ask yourself, does what you see appear to be awkward or does it illustrate comfort and balance? In relationship to being blocked, as opposed to its catchphrase, it symbolizes "I am not," as in "I am not secure" or "I am not grounded" or "I am not comfortable in this situation or circumstance." When this type of behavior or blocking is seen, depending on the circumstance, we want to try and find a way to open this behavior to allow the person to feel safe and secure in the situation. Should you ever find yourself trying to build or maintain rapport in a conversation with someone and you see blockage starting to surface, try changing the topic or giving the other person the opportunity to talk about something that interests them.

The **sacral chakra** is located just below the naval area and relates to the body's emotions, pleasures, and sensuality. Its affirmation and relationship catchphrase is "I feel." As with all open body language, we allow ourselves to remain unguarded and relaxed when we  feel trust and rapport with others. When pets lie on their backs and allow

 their stomachs to be rubbed, they expose the most vulnerable parts of their bodies. We humans are not too different in how we allow ourselves to be open or closed off when we feel threatened or guarded. Located just above the root chakra, the sacral chakra resides in the area of our lower abdomen, just above our groin. When blocked or a sense of discomfort is present, this area may also be covered with the hands/arms. Some individuals may have nervousness in the lower stomach region that creates a sense of not feeling well (mentally or physically). Because this area deals with emotions, pleasures, and sensuality, when it is blocked or disrupted, an individual may close themselves off to others, showing a lack of desire or passion to do anything regarding physical, mental, or sexual stimulation. For a visual image of this, imagine someone giving themselves a hug or caressing their lower abdomen area while seated or standing and covering this region. Some may even bend or fold over in a

leaning manner to express they are *not feeling well* or close up somewhat like a clam or almost in the fetal position, blocking this area when emotions are high. They may even make statements to the effect of *I don't feel like being bothered right now* or *I don't feel like talking.* In other words, there is an absence of desire. One key to this, if it is not expressed verbally, is to be aware of the nonverbal behavior being shown.

As I reflect on these first two chakras, one thing I have noticed within myself is when I go to any dental appointments, I feel as though I am in good hands with my dentist. Throughout all the years I have been a patient of his practice, he and his staff have not posed any concerns that would make me feel threatened even though I am not in control of the situation. As I enter the room and the assistant allows me to be seated and places the bib around my neck to cover my shirt, I am still somewhat relaxed. The assistant and I are usually engaged in casual conversation, discussing my day and how I have been, plans for vacation, and so on. They give me the eyewear and allow me to watch television, and then the dentist enters and does his initial meet and greet.

Once he begins to recline the seat, I am still feeling pretty good until the point when the seat is fully reclined and the overhead light comes on for him to look inside my mouth. I seem to always catch myself crossing my legs at the ankles and holding my clasped hands just below my belly button. I have often asked myself why I do this, and the truth is I am bit nervous. I'm nervous as to what may be found, what he has to do, how long the procedure will take, how long I will have to be in that position, and so on. I realize that I am in a vulnerable position, as all of my private regions are open and exposed if someone wanted to look at me, and I am not in a position of authority but of submission.

Covering myself with my hands provides a bit of comfort and relief. It allows me to self-soothe and not feel as exposed. I close and lock my legs at the ankles to try and stabilize myself and keep my feet from moving around as I am tense and holding myself together as best I can. From an overhead view, it would probably look like I am preparing to go down a water slide after receiving instructions from the person at the top of the ride. My mind thinks that the dentist and assistant are looking at me from the chest down, but in reality they are probably focused on what's going on inside of my mouth.

Energetically, the root and the sacral chakras feel threatened, so I go into protection mode because the root chakra is about grounding and comfort, and I am not grounded and not in a comfortable position. I can't get up and run away, so I must do something with my legs to try and have some sense of control. Rather than move them or let them dangle freely, the next best option is to lock them together for a sense of security. Second, the sacral chakra is about feeling as it relates to emotions, sensuality, and pleasures. In this situation, I don't feel secure as my private parts would be open and vulnerable, so I use my hands to conceal and protect this area. Every time I notice I am doing these things, it's interesting that I am doing them subconsciously and not purposely. Even when trying to uncover these areas and relax, I find myself going right back to the same position until the procedure is done and the chair is restored to the upright position.

The **solar plexus** is located in the upper abdomen area just above the belly button and relates to our self-esteem, willpower, and self-confidence. Its affirmation and relationship catchphrase is "I do." When an individual feels powerful or does power poses, such as standing in the Superman pose with  their hands on their hips, their stomach region is exposed. When one is feeling confident or secure while speaking with others, we see open hand gestures as there is no need to protect this area. When blocked, as opposed to its catchphrase "I do," it symbolizes "I don't," as in "I don't want to do this" or "I will not do this" or "I do what I want to do." Individuals when blocked may also exhibit behaviors of being quick to anger. This is best visualized as when someone crosses their arms across their lower chest/upper stomach region when confrontation occurs or when they feel threatened and put up their guard. This behavior can also be related to how open or suggestible a person is based on the posture of their arms. If they are relaxed with their arms open and apart, there is a greater chance of a successful outcome as opposed to having the arms crossed, which could indicate they are closed off and not as open to suggestions because they may feel a bit intimidated or hesitant to take any action. If the arms are crossed, the individual is usually creating a barrier between themselves and whomever they are interacting with, and this energetically protects them. This movement also allows them time to think strategically and consider their next move before making any decisions and opening themselves up for further conversation. This pose can also give the impression that one is trying to manipulate a conversation and may come across as selfish. Allowing them to have their say or giving them a voice is one of the first steps to creating movement of the arms. Getting a person to tell what they feel usually gets the hands moving and facilitates the loosening of the arms to lower their resistance.

Often, when I see this position with the arms crossed, I cannot help but think of a former employee I used to supervise. Each time I would call my members together for an emergency meeting and express that I had news to share in relation to some duty or action we had to take, this member would always stand up (if they were seated) and immediately cross their arms, covering their sacral area. They were usually open in their opinions concerning extra duties and assignments and would often comment that they did not want to do it or express why they felt we should not have to do it. It was interesting to see that even if they were given the floor to speak, they would maintain the crossing of the arms but allow one forearm to free flow as they spoke, and then it would immediately return to its original position. As long as they wished to contest and deliberate their thoughts, they remained rigid and closed. As I began to understand the relationship of this energetic block, I gave this member the opportunity to provide solutions and suggestions to allow them to show what they would like and what we could do to help instead of complaining about what should not be done. When I allowed them to act as a leader and gave them opportunities in a team lead position to describe how we could all benefit,

I noticed their body language would open more and the arms would gradually open as they had to be more expressive either to write stuff down or point out individuals and give instructions for their suggestions. It was great to see that by giving them a position to boost their self-esteem and empowering them in a role that demanded action, they had no other choice but to transition from being blocked, opposed, and guarded to taking positive action.

When crossing of the arms is seen, take note of the level of comfort in conjunction with the height of the shoulders and whether they are shrugged. Crossed arms in the solar plexus region with shrugged shoulders, coupled with a furrowed brow and a tucked chin, is indicative of negative energy present. If the arms appear relaxed and the conversation is pleasant, ask yourself if the area is blocked or if is this a position of comfort for them. Some people may also do this to warm themselves or generate heat if they are cold. Being observant to all parts of the conversation and the environment is key to preventing interpretation errors when reading others.

The **heart** is located just as it is named, within the center and heart area of the chest. It relates to and represents our ability to show love and compassion and is the bridge between the upper and lower chakras. It unites the individual with spiritual insight relating to consciousness, truth, and intuition. Its affirmation and relationship catchphrase is "I love." When open and when one has an emotional connection with something, we can often see the correlation with the hand touching the chest/heart area in extremely heartfelt situations. It assists us in bringing in or accepting love as well as being able to express it outwardly to others. It is not uncommon to see individuals speak of situations that demonstrate how much they love a friend, family member, or item while doing movements that allow the hand to touch their chest. These movements will also often show in the face and their tonality when speaking. Keep in mind, the touching of the chest/heart area can be soft and gentle or intense with emotion, such as when expressing anger. It all depends on the context and how it impacts the speaker. When blocked, on the other hand, it inhibits the ability to love or show love on a personal level. Be mindful and look for areas that lack congruency when people speak of things they claim they love without showing emotion.

The **throat chakra** is located in the throat area and relates and connects with our ability to communicate verbally with others. It directly correlates to our voice, what we will say, and how it will be presented. Its affirmation and relationship catchphrase is "I talk" or "I speak." We typically don't cover our throats during a conversation; however, there have been times I have seen individuals get frustrated or stressed while speaking and have a loss of words. This may at times accompany the lowering of the chin and placing the hand at the base of it, just below the lips, while covering the throat area, or even during the classic display of shock when someone perhaps receives bad news, and they put their hand over their open mouth and throat area representing "I am speechless" or "I don't know what to say." Also, when someone is verbally attacked, they may purposely cover their mouth and throat area to block what they want to communicate to avoid being harsh or abrupt. It could also be accompanied by an attempt to clear the throat before speaking or while being attacked by another. This is not uncommon to hear when someone is put on the spot and is stalling for time to collect their thoughts before speaking. It could be attributed to nervous energy channeled to the vocal cords under stress that need to relax before speaking.

The **third eye** is located in the center of the forehead, just above the

eyebrows and just below the hairline area. It relates to and represents our vision, imagination, and intuition. Its affirmation and relationship catchphrase is "I see." Often, when blocked or we cannot find the answers for insight, we may cover or rub our hands in this area to try and stimulate it so we can see what is missing. This could also be done after you realize you have been taken advantage of and are trying to determine how the situation happened or how it could have been avoided. In other words, our ability to "see" is blocked or blinded.

A few years ago, I became ill and had to be admitted to the hospital for observation. I was there for about a week before being released and sent home for recovery. Once I arrived home, it was time for some relaxation and healing. My wife and I started contacting some of the medical providers I needed to see for follow-up appointments to help me on my path to healing. Although I was fortunate to have insurance through my job, I knew bills would soon be on their way. I remember receiving a bill from the hospital some weeks later that had a breakdown of what my insurance company paid in comparison to what I owed. As soon as I saw the dollar amount I had to pay, I could not believe it. I remember lowering my head and immediately putting my hand on my forehead. I closed my eyes, exhaled deeply, and shook my head left and right as if to say "No, this can't be," trying to figure out how a one-week hospital stay could be close to twenty thousand dollars. I thought to myself, "How am I going to come up with this kind of money, and how long will it take me to pay this bill off?" I was trying to use my imagination to see what options I had available. Unfortunately, the answers didn't come right away as I was under severe stress. Eventually, I calmed myself down and focused on what I needed to accomplish. As I closed my eyes, I had a bird's-eye view of myself making payment arrangements and designing options that would be for my greater good to help me pay off my medical debts. It is very interesting and insightful to note that when the third eye is activated, the two eyes on our face are not being used. Our eyes on the outside are only used to see what is in our present and in the moment. The visions and insight we receive from the third eye cannot be seen with the outside eyes but only internally. The third eye gives us clarity and focus and allows us to see our past and future to bring the awareness that we need for purpose, direction, and wisdom.

Some also attribute to this chakra our practical ability to avoid being misled and to see trouble and opportunities that are right in front of us. Think about a time when you saw someone trying to take advantage of another, and for whatever reason, you saw the negativity from a mile away, but the other person couldn't seem to see it at all. At times, people can be temporary "blinded" by their emotions and therefore unable to think clearly or reasonably. Even though they can physically see, they choose to ignore a person's flaws or other concerns that might help them avoid a negative outcome as curiosity pushes them to try to fulfill their inner desires regardless of the consequences. This can show up in a person's life as getting into a troubled relationship and refusing to leave or even making impulse purchases without doing enough research because the salesperson was attractive or the opportunity seemed too good to pass up.

The **crown chakra** is at the top of the head and pertains to our awareness, wisdom, and intelligence. Its affirmation and relationship catchphrase is "I understand." When one has encountered extreme disbelief or something unimag-  inable, they may place their hands on top of their head in awe or shock; this may also be accompanied by the expression "Oh my goodness." This would be the opposite of its catchphrase, representing "I don't understand." This could be visualized as a person making or missing the game-winning shot at the buzzer. They illustrate their emotion and expression as they have done the unthinkable, impossible, or unimaginable. Those experiencing high levels of stress and blockage may exhibit this expression as they seek guidance or wisdom to figure out how to get out of their stressful situation or even ask themselves how they originally got into it. This expression is not the same as having one's hands interlaced on the back of the head, as though cradling it for comfort when sitting with the feet kicked back while relaxing on the couch. The meanings are not the same. When a parent or caretaker is holding an infant, we typically see them place a hand at the back and base of the infant's head for support and comfort. When we lie down on our back, we will often support the base of the head for comfort. When individuals are sitting at a desk and kick their feet up, you will often see the hands behind the head with the elbows extended in an outward display representing comfort, confidence, and achievement, as opposed to at the top of the head, which represents disbelief or lack of understanding.

In 2018, I watched a video containing body camera footage of Chris Watts, who was convicted of killing his pregnant wife and two children in Frederick, Colorado. The body camera footage starts with the officer walking into the residence of a neighbor who had video cameras that recorded the outside street areas, hoping to gain some insight into what happened the evening the wife and daughters went missing. Chris looks at the television screen as his neighbor begins to show video footage with the outside of their houses. He briefly turns around and has his back toward the screen; he exhales deeply and then returns to face it and puts both hands on top of his head. Seconds after putting his hands on his head, he begins to rock from side to side and pulls both of his lips inside his mouth as everyone is watching the screen looking for evidence. Something gets Chris's attention (perhaps his phone), and he releases one hand to check it while the other remains on top of his head. As soon as he finishes, he returns his hand right back to his head. He is taking deeper breaths and his eyes flutter quickly, and when the officer begins to speak, he turns and faces him. Chris continues to rock from side to side with his hands on top of his head and his lips pulled inward.

He does not release his hands from his head until he begins to speak to the officer and inadvertently hits his sunglasses, which fall over the top of his eyes.

What can be deduced from the body camera footage is that Chris was in disbelief that someone possibly had footage of him carrying his wife's body out of the house. The hands on top of the head illustrates that the crown chakra was being affected due to feeling shock or awe. He was more than likely in disbelief that this was happening. The root chakra was also being affected, which was demonstrated as he rocked from side to side because he was not grounded and was not comfortable in the situation. He couldn't leave the room and get out of the area, so his sympathetic nervous system did what it knows best to handle the fight-or-flight circumstance. The energy in his body was rampant, and relaxation was the furthest thing from his mind. The interesting thing about the entire situation is that Chris probably didn't even realize what he was doing, just as many people are also unaware of what they are doing when they are energetically out of balance.

As referenced earlier, success can be measured in several ways, and so can one's progress in learning to recognize body language. Depending on your trade, profession, and daily involvement with others, a variety of methods can assist you in recognizing body language and facial expressions. The same is also proven to be successful in law enforcement interactions to defuse dangerous encounters before they escalate. In any event, do not be afraid to integrate any special skills you already possess to enhance the information you learn while reading this book.

The Takeaway

- If the first chakra—Root (I am, sense of grounding, survival, security)—appears to be blocked, provide words of security and let them know that it's OK if they don't know or have an answer/solution to what is being talked about at the moment. Scattered energy is running throughout the body, and you may need to change the topic to get the body back to a relaxed state.

Let them know how strong they are for talking about whatever the issue or challenge is in front of them.

- If the second chakra—Sacral (I feel, creativity, sexuality)—appears to be blocked, ask them what they love to do or what drives them and makes them passionate in life. Allow them to express themselves in a creative way without judgment. Create pathways that show you trust them and that feeling can be reciprocated.

- If the third chakra—Solar Plexus (I do, self-esteem, willpower)—appears to be blocked, let the person know they have value and their words/actions are worthy of being expressed. Provide insight to help alleviate the doubt, disbelief, or rejection that keeps them from feeling strong and confident.

- If the fourth chakra—Heart (I love, compassion)—appears to be blocked, allow them to feel a sense of being loved (e.g., you love their ideas, you would love to hear what they have to say). Show them that you welcome whatever it is they want to express with an open heart and open mind. Let it be known that fear of failure or whatever is holding them back from their past should not be a part of their future. Express that you are grateful for them sharing their experiences.

- If the fifth chakra—Throat (I speak, voice, communication)—appears to be blocked, give them an opportunity to speak. Be interested in what they have to say, ask them to speak honestly, and show no judgment. Ask them to speak their truth and say what they truly feel about a situation. As they will probably be a bit shy or anxious, don't press too hard but get them involved in conversations as an integral part with a voice. Compliment them on their ability to speak in a clear, concise manner.

- If the sixth chakra—Third Eye (I see, intuition, imagination)—appears to be blocked, allow insight for them to trust their path and their decisions. If they feel their situation is unattainable, let them know it is OK to feel confused and without direction, but also try to tap into what they would like to happen to help overcome what is troubling them. Share with them that whatever is blocking them is a great opportunity to grow and learn.

- If the seventh chakra—Crown (I believe, higher consciousness)—appears to be blocked, try to assist them in being open-minded by giving options to see things in a different light that can coexist with their own way of thinking as well as their sense of purpose. Let them see the ability to live in the moment while trying to let go of troubling attachments to seek wisdom from their higher self.

Chapter Six

MICRO EXPRESSION BASICS

**Gestures and facial expressions do indeed
communicate, as anyone can prove by
turning off the sound on a television
set and asking watchers to characterize
the speakers from the picture alone.**
~ PETER FARB

The face holds a wealth of information about a person and is one of the first parts of the body that we observe to identify with others. One of the primary reasons for observing a person's face is to first determine whether we recognize the individual as a friend or an acquaintance, or if we will identify them as a stranger or one who presents a danger to us.

In addition, the face can be a valuable tool in recognizing specific qualities or characteristics of others. In some cultures, wrinkles, shapes, and other markings on the face are used to assist with evaluating a person's health and well-being. These lines or wrinkles on the face are typically indicative of expressions that have been made frequently throughout a person's life, which could represent how they felt emotionally during specific times. After all, if one were to make a particular facial expression and hold it for several seconds or even minutes at a time, the skin would retract and conform back to its original position. With this thought in mind, when one sees a wrinkle or line engraved in the skin that is not the product of a wound or injury, it is usually the result of a long-term expression that developed over time via muscle memory repetition. When I reminisce on my childhood days, I remember my mom telling me that I had better stop making certain faces or it would get stuck like that. While my face did not actually get stuck from those playful movements, there is some truth in the idea that the face shows areas in which specific expressions are made, which brings us to micro expressions.

I remember being on patrol one afternoon when I saw a driver and passenger in a vehicle approach and pass me, and neither of them were wearing their seat belt. I activated my blue lights and executed a U-turn in the roadway, and the vehicle immediately sped up to get away from me. It took me a few seconds to accelerate, and as I rounded the curve they had just passed, I saw them turn off onto a side street in a neighborhood. I followed them, and as I began to close the gap, they pulled into the driveway of a vacant residence and stopped. I got out of my car, made my approach, and told the driver who I was and the reason for the traffic stop. I asked for his license and registration. He patted himself on the top of his thighs and by his rear pockets and advised me that he didn't have either item in his possession. He was very polite and appeared to be mildly nervous. I got out my notepad and asked for his name, date of birth, and other pertinent information, which he gave me without delay. I then looked at the passenger and asked for his name and date of birth. He opened his eyes wide, raised his eyebrows very briefly, and then just stared at me with his mouth partially open as though he was in shock. I recall asking him if he knew his name, since he appeared confused, and he stated, "That was my name." At that point, I was the one confused and said, "Excuse me? What do you mean that was your name?" He then told me that the driver had given me *his* name. I looked back at the driver, who held his head down and pulled his lips in and downward momentarily as I asked who he was. He told me his real name, and I asked why he had given me his friend's name. He said it was because his license was suspended, and he thought there might be a warrant out for his arrest. He said that was also the reason he had tried to outrun me when he saw me turn around in the roadway. He indicated that he had asked his friend if he had a valid license before I approached the car, to which the friend replied yes, and he got his information to give to me, not knowing that I was going to need the passenger's name as well. A further check revealed the driver did in fact have a suspended license, and he was given a citation for the violations. Had I not truly been paying attention to the movements of the face, I'm guessing that the passenger's silence and delayed response would have led to more in-depth questioning, but more interesting was the fact that neither of them could shield their faces' natural responses to surprise and sadness. This is one example of the significance of recognizing micro expressions.

A micro expression is a brief, involuntary facial movement caused by an individual's internal emotion. These expressions are brief, meaning they typically last for a half second or less, and they are easily missed if one is not looking for or able to recognize them. Not only are they brief, but they can also be tiny and subtle, hence the word "micro." They expose leakage of a true emotion that many people will wish to conceal or suppress, and quite often, the individual is not even aware they have displayed the expression.

One unfortunate aspect of evaluating a micro expression is that you cannot ask an individual to repeat it. Once it has been displayed, you more than likely will not see it again, even if you repeat the statement or question that triggered the initial response. However, there are ways to re-question or ask for additional information to attempt to elicit the same or other related facial expressions displayed during your initial conversation.

As seen in most photos or when a facial expression is held for a longer period than a micro expression, it is considered a macro expression. A macro expression typically lasts from half a second to four seconds.

We see these expressions quite often in our daily interactions as others are usually not trying to conceal them. These are shown when we want to express our joy or happiness, our frustration or pain, or our dislike of specific items without trying to hide how we feel. With that being said, let's take a moment to review how we came to understand micro expressions as we know them today.

Micro expressions were initially discovered in 1966 by Ernest Haggard and Kenneth Isaacs while they were scanning motion picture films of clinical reviews. These films were searched for nonverbal communications between the therapist and the patient. As they reviewed the films, they found it beneficial to observe the patients at different interval speeds, in addition to watching them in silence and backward motion, as opposed to the normal twenty-four frames per second.

As a result, they could see dramatic changes in a patient's face within different film frames. At the time, Haggard and Isaacs referred to these as micromomentary expressions (MMEs). A few years later, in 1969, Paul Ekman would take this study further as he ventured to Papua New Guinea to study the Fore people's nonverbal communication and behavior.

Due to the Fore people's isolation, cultural differences, and what may be considered antiquated ways of living, Ekman wanted to see if they behaved in the same ways as others in different parts of the world. His research determined that they shared the same universal traits and emotions with others worldwide.

During the past fifty years, other researchers have continued to study and grow this area of interest in behavior and emotions and extend their training and experience across the globe.

These expressions (micro and macro) are useful in recognizing authentic as well as potentially false, exaggerated emotions that are not genuinely created. Researchers have identified seven basic micro expressions that are generated from emotions created within the body. They are happiness, sadness, anger, fear, surprise, disgust, and contempt. Let's look at each of these in greater detail.

Happiness

Happiness is a sign of emotion that expresses pleasure or joy. It signifies that all is well at that moment, and the person demonstrating the expression is relaxed and not under duress or in anguish. Typically, we consider smiling the standard sign of a person's happiness.

When viewed directly from the front, a genuine smile should be symmetrical (or evenly structured) on both sides of the face. The cheeks are extended, and the lines or wrinkles surrounding the lips' outer corners are arched and almost form a circle about the lower portion of the face. Depending on their strength, comfort, and happiness level, some individuals may show their teeth while others may not.

It should be noted that when a polite smile is given that does not reflect true happiness, the display will vanish rather quickly. The corners of the mouth and cheeks rise and fall almost immediately, since the expression is controlled rather than genuine. A true feeling of happiness takes time to fade away, as the joy and excitement come from the heart, and it takes a moment for the feeling to pass. Think about a moment in your past when you were truly happy, and notice as you smile reflecting on the memory how long the emotion lasts before your cheeks begin to relax. The duration will be longer than if you just raise and lower your cheeks, pretending to be happy and then releasing the muscles in your face.

When happiness is displayed during conversation, the topic that was referenced can be noted to utilize at a later time in an effort to maintain the level of rapport.

Sadness

Sadness is expressed when a person feels disheartened or unhappy. It is seen predominantly in times of grief or sorrow. It is probably best interpreted as the opposite of happiness and is usually denoted as an upside-down smile or better yet, a frown.

As sadness is expressed, the inner eyebrows are brought closer together and raised toward the middle of the forehead. This is a highly reliable sign that many people are not able to generate on demand. The eyes will usually be softened in their appearance at the outer corners and above the upper eyelid. The face may seem expressionless as the muscles between the eyebrows are pulled inward, doing a majority of the work and allowing other areas to relax, and there may be a frown or lowering of the lip corners. A slight rise in the chin may also be present with the frown. In small children, the lower lip may poke outward in a pouting behavior.

When speaking to an individual who is exhibiting sadness, one must be mindful of their own actions to avoid creating unnecessary distance or a break in rapport. Being empathetic or comforting to someone while they are feeling depressed or unhappy can continue to build rapport and strengthen a relationship.

Anger

Anger can be displayed when an individual is upset, frustrated, furious, and even irritated. We typically associate this facial expression with a person who is mad, highly frustrated, or extremely bothered. However, when the lowering of the brows is present, which is sometimes accompanied by squinting, an individual may simply be focusing intently or displaying a brief moment of confusion or uncertainty rather than anger. Ultimately, the signals displayed should be ruled in or out depending on the context in which the expression was seen.

In recognizing the signs of anger, it should be noted there are several indicators and factors. Usually, anger is identified with a furrowing or lowering of the brow over the top of the eyes. For some, the area inside the eyebrows may crease, and parallel vertical lines or wrinkles may be seen, similar to the number eleven (11).

The focus of the eyes is specific and direct and is typically fixated on or toward the target of the anger. The bottoms of the eyelids may raise slightly, showing intensity, or there may be a cold stare that some would refer to as "the stare of death" or "if looks could kill."

Another expression that may be seen in conjunction with the eyes is a tightening of the lips. Often, when we humans hide our lips, it is to keep our words in our mouths so as not to say something harmful, hateful, or hurtful. Chin juts (a quick raising motion of the chin toward the target) may occur but can be easily overlooked if one is not trained to watch for them. Finally, some individuals may clench their teeth, and contraction may be seen in the lower jaw area just below and slightly forward of the ear.

It is important to recognize that several of these traits may be seen in conjunction with one another, but they may also be seen separately, depending on the individual and their level of control. Typically, the most reliable areas for noticing anger will be the eyebrow region with the furrowing of the brow as well as fury being demonstrated in the eyes. This sign should not be confused with concentration, which displays itself as a sense of focus and may appear as a squint. The duration of an anger micro expression will also be shorter than that of focus or concentration, as the former is done in an attempt to conceal the emotion, while the latter demonstrates that one is trying to gather more information.

When recognizing that anger is present, at times it may be beneficial to allow a person to verbally vent and release the pressure they are holding, as long as it does not become physical. Allowing individuals to speak about the matter and offering suggestions presents a sense of caring and understanding.

Fear

Fear is displayed when an individual is scared or afraid. However, this expression may be confused with surprise because they share some similarities. Fortunately, with a trained eye, one can distinguish between the two by evaluating the circumstances at hand and whether the emotion was appropriate.

The first sign of recognizing fear is that the eyebrows appear stressed and tense. They are raised above the eyelids with a likeness of surprise but are straighter in comparison. The eyes are widened to the point that more of the whites of the eyes are visible. The mouth open is also representative of fear, with the mouth corners stretching outward to the sides of the face.

Depending on whether the neck is visible, when the mouth corners spread sideways, the neck muscles may also be seen contracting to protect themselves from harm or danger.

It is important to recognize when seeing this expression that not all signs and indications may be visible or occur simultaneously. For example, the eyes may widen and the eyebrows react while the mouth remains closed.

If a sense of fear is seen, ask yourself what was said or done just before the expression was displayed. Reassurance will be needed to calm the individual expressing fear. When a sense of fear is shown, it telegraphs that protection or comfort is desired. If this occurs in a sales situation, perhaps the price given was too high, and it will be crucial to try and counter this reaction quickly by allowing the person to provide feedback or share their thoughts on what might be a reasonable price.

Surprise

 Surprise is typically displayed when a person sees, hears, or experiences something that creates a temporary sense of shock or amazement. It is brief in its display and may be accompanied by a different emotion displayed directly afterward. For example, a person may come home to find an entire living room full of guests for a surprise birthday party. When everyone yells "Surprise!" upon their arrival, they may display an emotion of happiness and smile. However, if they had no desire for a party and wanted to be alone, they may then flash a sign of anger.

When surprise is displayed, the eyebrows will typically rise toward the top of the head, but they will have more of an arc, rounded, or semicircular shape as opposed to when exhibiting fear. The forehead wrinkling is more relaxed as the stress level is not as high as that of fear.

The eyes may also widen, and the whites of the eyes may be readily visible.

If the mouth should open, it is also more relaxed than in a fearful expression, with a drop in the lower jaw or chin region. The mouth may appear to demonstrate a sense of awe or be circular in shape like the letter "O," as if to state, "Oh my!"

Expressions of surprise are quite often seen in general conversations to demonstrate "That's interesting" or "This topic I'm talking about is interesting," with the expectation of maintaining attention span. It should also be noted that not every trait listed here may appear, as one may only exhibit eyebrow and eyelid flashes without showing the opening of their mouth, or vice versa.

This trait of raising the eyebrows and opening the eyes can also be seen by individuals trying to promote interest and show their delight or sense of astonishment when explaining details about a particular circumstance. Depending on the context, it may be seen when one recalls a previous situation they were in, and they are back in the moment and emphasizing how they felt at that time.

Disgust

Disgust is displayed when an individual has an emotional sense of extreme dislike or distaste for something. The thought of something being unpleasant or repulsive, such as a sight or smell, can also trigger the expression.

A good example of this could be imagining a half-eaten dead animal on the side of the roadway and the smell it produces. Another example could be opening a milk carton that has been unrefrigerated for a couple of days and smelling the spoiled milk.

When disgust is displayed, the nose is often wrinkled, and the areas on its sides (on the bottom near the nostrils) will also show movement. There may also be some wrinkling along the top (bridge) of the nose and just under the inner corners of the eyes.

Depending on the individual and the intensity of the emotion, the upper lip may rise in conjunction with the wrinkling alongside the nose. As opposed to the wrinkles or lines on the face when a person smiles, which are semicircular or outward toward the sides of the face extending from the cheeks, these wrinkles are viewed up and down the length of the face.

Contempt

Contempt is an interesting expression as it may possess two different meanings. First, it can signify a person is feeling superior to someone or something and show disdain or a lack of respect for an individual or even a situation. To the untrained eye, it can appear as a smile; however, it is asymmetrical. When viewed directly, head-on or face-to-face with an individual, it should be noted that only one side of the mouth will raise higher than the other.

Second, contempt may be seen as slow, controlled eye-rolling to express dislike for what was seen or heard. This could be done with or without the asymmetrical pull of one corner of the mouth. Either way, it could potentially be followed by a deep inhale and exhale expressing the lack of respect as well.

Because contempt has two different meanings, it is essential to understand why it is being displayed to make an informed decision on how to interpret it. For example, if a supervisor tells their staff members they are receiving pay raises this year and an individual leaks (displays) contempt, could it be because they have not received a pay raise in years and are skeptical?

Here's another example: an employee is accused of stealing money from the workplace, and when asked about it, they leak a sign of contempt. Could this be due to the staff member feeling offended that they were asked such a question, or is it because they took the money and are aware that the interviewer is clueless and they might get away with the theft?

It is important to remember that displays of contempt in relationships can be detrimental, and studies indicate that they are also the biggest predictor of divorce. When an individual expresses contempt, they are expressing an inward emotion, as they may feel as though the other person is attempting to overpower them and demonstrate authority over them, and the expression is leaked to express their lack of appreciation for this. Take a moment and think about a time that a loved one or person in authority made statements directly to you that you *felt* were attacks on your intelligence, your appearance, your mannerisms, or your integrity. Whether they were intentionally trying to hurt you or just telling the truth in their own way, you may have taken offense at their statements.

Leaking contempt is a natural response when trying to control our behavior to suppress our lack of respect for what was said to us. However, if you are talking to someone (spouse, significant other, friend, colleague, or potential business partner) and see signs of contempt, recognize this is an emotion that expresses how they *feel* based on their interpretation and perception of a negative judgment toward them (or possibly affiliated with them somehow), which can create resentment. Noticing this behavior should spark the need to be mindful about our choice of words to illustrate the opposite of contempt, which is words that portray appreciation and respect.

When viewing micro expressions, it is essential to focus on the structure and movements of the face. More importantly, this task should be done without appearing as if you are staring at someone. For this reason, having a baseline is worth its weight in gold in establishing relaxed or normal behavior. If time was not taken at the onset of a conversation to recognize the face in a relaxed or neutral setting with nonthreatening questions or remarks, there is a strong probability that you may misinterpret a person's facial expressions.

Unfortunately, if a micro expression is missed, there is no direct means of rewinding the emotion to see it again. However, suppose it is suspected that a micro expression was missed. In that case, one should follow up with a related question to see if another emotional expression is brought forth that coincides with what may have been missed. Wait and observe between four and seven seconds for a response. It is expected that any reoccurrence of an emotion will happen during that time frame. If not, there is no need to worry. There will be plenty of opportunities to see more reactions during your interactions with others.

At this point, you have been introduced to the energetic aspects of what occurs internally when the body is affected as well as how micro and macro expressions can aid in determining an individual's emotional state. These two skills will prove to be useful in your life as you now possess information that many people are not aware of and don't know how to recognize when it's displayed in front of them. As we move forward to the next chapter, you will be introduced to the language of the body and how certain movements and gestures relate to our behavior.

Chapter Seven

BODY LANGUAGE BASICS

We can know a person by observing his behavior, understanding the reasons for his actions and ascertaining his intentions. If we do this, how can we not know him?
~ CONFUCIUS

The ability to read body language is a skill everyone can acquire as long as they are willing to learn. In certain respects, some body language movements are easily interpreted. For example, if a person is clutching their chest with one or both hands and looking down toward their chest with a grimace, we may assume they don't feel well and possibly have chest pain.

Or consider a person who buries their face in their cupped hands while looking downward and then massages their temples. We more than likely believe they are feeling stress, frustration, pain, or even anxiety.

We each have our own body language actions, and because of the common movements we share, we recognize and compare the behaviors of others with our own. Unfortunately, since we see and do these behaviors repeatedly, they are an everyday occurrence and may not have a significant impact when needed the most.

It becomes the norm to see people speak with their hands, display emotions with their faces, and change their body movements and positions while standing or sitting, and thus it does not have much bearing on the conversation.

When training one's eyes to master the ability to recognize specific movements—subtle changes and behaviors in conjunction with speech patterns and analysis—it is possible to understand all facets of an individual for what they really are. As we begin this chapter, we will discuss the aspects of body language as they apply to social settings and the surrounding in which they are used.

Proxemics

Proxemics is a significant ingredient in the communication platform. It is based on the study of *space* between two or more individuals. Edward T. Hall first coined this term during a study that involved people from different cultures, as he observed that they do not all attach the same meaning to specific distances. For example, I have personally experienced that when meeting some people from different cultures, they prefer to shake hands, hug, and give a kiss on the cheek when first meeting. They treat you as a close friend or like family even though they don't know you very well. With other cultures, distance is preferred, and a handshake from a distance is the preferred method as they do not want to get too close to you.

In nonverbal communication, boundaries are often set (based on comfort levels) without a person having to speak up when someone gets too close, which is often referred to as *invading one's personal space.* If one feels another is too close, they may initially respond by observing to see if they recognize the individual as a friend or foe.

If it is still felt they are too close, additional space is created. Some may give a look of confusion to nonverbally ask, "Why are you so close to me?" As a last resort, if the other person does not take the hint, the individual may voice their concerns openly to advise the other party to back up, or they may decide to simply walk away to avoid the situation altogether.

Studies have shown that we have four zones of proxemics. These are intimate, personal, social, and public. Each zone is defined by specific measurements that indicate an individual's comfort level.

The intimate measure of distance is from zero to eighteen inches. This zone is labeled *intimate* due to its closeness to one's body, as we usually do not allow people to get this close to us unless we have an extreme level of comfort with them. This intimate space is typically reserved for partners in relationships or members of our core and immediate family. We usually see this with individuals holding hands, kissing, hugging, sharing a phone screen, and other personal interactions.

The *personal zone* of proxemics is measured from eighteen inches to four feet. This area is usually designated for our immediate friends and those within our circle of trust. Be mindful not to invade this area too quickly when first meeting someone and trying to build rapport with them. Even though we may want to establish a personal relationship, that does not mean they are ready to do so, and they may be offended and guarded. The initial "barrier breaker" to cross this threshold will usually be a handshake when greeting someone. Afterward, the retreat to the social zone should be taken unless the person allows or welcomes you to come closer.

The **social zone** is from four to ten feet. Our everyday encounters with individuals we regard as acquaintances are usually maintained within this range. In 2020, due to the COVID-19 pandemic, "social distancing" provisions were created that mandated a six-foot distance to try to

prevent the spread of the virus. When first meeting others, this is typically where we want to be. This can be seen in grocery store aisles, checkout lines, and even in office settings such as cubicles or some meetings. As a bond or level of trust and rapport is developed, one may notice the zone shortening to share information more or less on a personal level.

The **public zone** is indicated as ten feet and beyond in distance. This zone is labeled *public* and is representative of its name.

In our public interactions with strangers, those we do not know or feel any immediate connection with, we feel most comfortable keeping our distance from them. This is typically seen in shopping malls, public parks, and waiting rooms when enough seating is available. Even in these public gatherings, you can easily take note to see who is interacting in intimate, personal, and social zones.

As you continue your study of body language and micro expressions, be mindful and aware of which proxemic zone you are operating in. If you are too far away, you are not being socially congruent to hold a conversation.

The key is being self-aware and recognizing that individuals need space. Just as you do not want a complete stranger bombarding you, others will feel the same way.

The Head

The head is one portion of the body that communicates a substantial amount of information. It houses the brain, which aids in transmitting information to the rest of the body. Four areas of the head receive and transmit information from the senses: ears for hearing, mouth for tasting, nose for smelling, and eyes for seeing. During most verbal and nonverbal communication, a significant amount of our focus will be on a person's face or head.

When the head is positioned directly front-facing an individual and the chin is raised ever so slightly, it indicates that an individual is proud or confident. At times, this may be seen in conjunction with the shoulders being held back while the chest is moved slightly forward. This also gives insight to the saying "Keep your head up" when someone is depressed or feeling a sense of failure to encourage them to stay positive, confident, and persevere even during hard times and adversity.

Holding one's head straight downward while looking toward the floor with a slight slump may indicate shame or guilt. This trait is often shown when someone has done something wrong or potentially demonstrated a lack of competence, and the issue is being addressed. The individual is expressing they feel bad or ashamed for what was done and cannot look the other person in the eye or view the situation head-on as they feel some remorse.

This trait may be accompanied by a micro or macro expression of sadness, which would further validate the interpretation. This action may also be seen in some pets (such as dogs) when being scolded for performing a negative action, such as relieving themselves in the house.

A head turned or leaned sideways about thirty degrees (either right or left) but still front-facing can exhibit an interest or question about what someone is saying to them. The ear closest to the person speaking will typically be the listener's dominant ear. They are "lending an ear" to hear everything that is being said, as it is important to them and they do not want to miss it.

A person's head, when looking downward and slightly to the side (left or right) with the eyes facing in the same direction, may indicate an internal conversation, pondering, or thought concerning a previous action.

Depending on the intensity of this internal conversation, facial expressions may be exhibited to indicate concentration to ensure they are correct in their thought.

The Triple Nod

A single nod by itself is acknowledgment of a person's presence that shows a form of respect; this can be a head tilt upward or a single nod downward. Depending on the familiarity of the people involved, a head nod in an upward direction can be indicative of "What's up?" and the head nod downward is showing respect while saying hi. For myself, I usually do an upward single nod, especially for my close friends when I see them, and when meeting strangers or toward my elders, I give a downward nod as if to say, "How are you doing?" As I recall from watching movies like westerns or from back in the '50s and '60s, it was not uncommon to also see men give a downward nod as they grabbed and tipped their hats to show respect when engaging with or first meeting a woman.

As this gesture is usually done by males, it should be noted that the upward nod is slight in its movement unless with familiar parties. Performing an upward nod too aggressively while saying "What's up?" can potentially come across as a chin jut or challenge to another male and may cause immediate friction. Because of this, if I meet another male around my age range, I will either give a very slight upward nod (about half of what I do with friends) to show mutual respect or a quick downward nod.

When engaging with others, one effective way to measure whether a person is paying attention to you, as well as for you to display you are paying attention to them, is the *triple nod*. The triple nod consists of three small, quick, equally performed nods that are used to nonverbally indicate "I'm listening." This is a subconscious action as it occurs without a person having to consciously think to do it. As people are engaged with you and listening, take note to see if they are doing these three head nods as you speak. The triple nod illustrates interest, indicating they like what they hear and don't mind hearing more of what you have to say.

If the nods become rapid and are accompanied by "Uh-huh, uh-huh," this can indicate impatience. The listener may be pressed for time or losing interest, and they want you to hurry up and say what you need to say. The movement may appear to be as though they are "bobble-heading," moving up and down at a faster rate than normal, which should be a great indicator to either wrap up your conversation, give them an opportunity to speak, or change the topic of discussion to maintain their interest.

The Eyes

The eyes provide a great amount of information when speaking to someone as they can be used in conjunction with micro expressions to provide directions (left, right, up, down) and show interest or possible stress. The upper and lower eyelids can convey micro expressions indicating emotions such as anger, fear, and surprise. Squinting can also indicate concentration on what a person is relaying or focus on an object.

The pupils may be a valuable source of information to some, as pupil dilation can be strongly correlated with stress. In addition to pupil dilation, there may be an increase in heart rate and sweating. Pupils dilate when we need to see better. This will typically come directly from one's sympathetic nervous system activating to protect and assist the body in a flight, fight, or freeze situation.

It should be noted that pupil dilation also occurs when people see things they find appealing. The pupils increase in diameter to accept more light to capture what is important for the viewer to see. This action of the eye can be compared to that of a camera lens when taking photos. The wider the aperture or opening of the lens, the more light is absorbed to capture and store what is seen by the photographer. This can also be seen in cats as their pupils will often widen when they are focused on attacking or looking at something of interest to them.

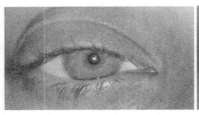 

Touching the Nose

Touching or rubbing the nose is one of a few motions that are often construed as a sign of deception. This age-old myth is exemplified by the fictional character Pinocchio, as it was indicated his nose would grow when he told a lie. This theory would prove to be inaccurate, as there is not any one definitive sign of deception known to man. However, touching the nose may provide information that indicates some level of stress is involved and the person may be rubbing it to assist in pacifying themself. This could be due to some of the erectile tissues in the nose being stimulated, which may affect the need to allow or restrict air flow. When this is seen, the situation must be evaluated further before assuming someone is being deceptive.

One also needs to be mindful of what was being discussed during the contact. If it happened at random times during the conversation or during silence, it could indicate that the person's nose was merely itching, or they had some other nasal issue. In other words, the situation would have to be monitored and looked at holistically to determine the frequency of touches and what was being discussed at the time of the action.

The Mouth

 The mouth is highly regarded in communication as it provides verbal messages to the listener. This, in conjunction with outward body language, helps express the full meaning of what is being relayed. Through the mouth, differences in tone, pitch, and rate of speech are delivered throughout the conversation. These can be very useful in determining believability and maintaining interest in a conversation.

The tone of voice refers to the voice's character during a message. It relates to the emotion and how it is expressed when a person speaks. This can best be explained as "It's not what you say but how you say it." It can often be seen as subtle, direct, or even rude, depending on how the receiver acknowledges what is said. If someone's tone is altered, this illustrates that there has been an imbalance in some aspect of the conversation from what it was at the beginning.

Pitch is "how high" or "how low" the message being spoken is presented. The pitch is important as it creates excitement, interest, or calmness while communicating with someone. An example of a monotone pitch would be a robotic style of speech, which is not varied and carries the same volume level throughout. Pitch can indicate an increase of stress, as when someone is asked if they did something and objects to the question. They may use a strong high pitch to answer "No!," "What?!," or "Why would I do that?" that is readily noticed in their voice.

Rate refers to how fast or slow a person speaks during a conversation. In body language or an interview-type setting, one would want to see if the speech rate speeds up while the pitch is lowered, which could indicate that someone is trying to make their speech more difficult to understand, possibly a sign of deception. This could also be reversed as a person may slow down their rate and raise their tone, indicating a more aggressive approach to intimidate the listener or to emphasize their point to indicate the seriousness of what they are saying.

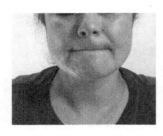 The mouth also provides us with a visible image of the lips, which are useful in detecting stress as well as micro expressions. The lips are typically visible as they protrude outwardly at rest, but they may begin to pull inward during times of stress, anger, or when tension is building within.

This is often highly visible when one is stressed and may want to openly voice their opinion, but they decide to hold their words back and bite their tongue (or their lips, in this instance).

The lips may be pressed together and appear hidden. Other signs of stress, such as deep breaths, shaking of the leg, etc., may accompany this action. This is a good indicator for validating an unwanted increase in stress or anger. Because of this, I like to say, "When the lips begin to hide, there's tension building inside."

The Chin

In body language, the chin relays a great deal of information based on the circumstances being presented. In Chinese face reading, the chin relates to our willpower and is also used to assist in determining one's stubbornness depending on its size and structure. Willpower relates to our ability to control our thoughts and actions, and therefore it makes sense that the chin, when seen in conjunction with specific hand placements, relates to thinking or evaluation.

Thumb to Chin—Showing Interest

When the thumb is placed under the chin and pointed toward the throat with the supporting fingers curled and closed just in front of the chin below the bottom lip, this shows that a person is in thinking mode and is paying attention. In this position, the index finger may or may not be covering the mouth or lips. Be mindful of where the person is looking as they may appear to be intently focused straight ahead on what the speaker or item they are observing is being analyzed. They may also appear to briefly or momentarily look up or downward towards specific sides of their body as they may be processing internal thoughts or conversation related to what is being evaluated. It is not uncommon to see the elbow of the hand resting under the chin  placed on the opposite arm's wrist, as it will usually be used for support as it crosses the belly region. In this position, the mouth (if covered), the solar plexus as well as the throat, energetically, are all temporarily blocked and guarded. This makes sense since when this position is shown, the person is not speaking—they are evaluating what, if anything, needs to be said and exerting their willpower by holding a stance to show they don't have to say or do anything at the moment unless they opt to. If the opposite arm is not available, the hand under the chin may be supported with the elbow resting on a table or even the leg of the person thinking, planning, or deciding. In each of these circumstances, it is important to note that the head itself is not solely supported by the thumb and fingers; they merely complement each other.

If the thumb and index finger begin to move from the relaxed or motionless state and shift a bit sideways to rub the chin in a downward or slight forward motion, this shows the person is moving from the listening and evaluation phase to making a calculated decision about what has been presented to them. If you are trying to make a sale or close a business deal, this would be the time to drive home all the most important aspects that would resonate with the person in front of you, as you have their undivided attention.

Another form of showing interest can be seen with the thumb under the chin at the rear of the jawline with the index finger pointing up and running alongside the cheek or maybe resting on the side of a nostril. The person's thumb will be just below or slightly in front of their ear. The other fingers will be curled in a closed position and also running alongside the cheek. Once again, the arm may be resting on the supporting arm as mentioned earlier, but the head is not solely supported by the thumb. The individual is only showing a connection for the thought process as the hand can be moved back and forth effortlessly and returned during conversation without the head being affected.

Palm under Chin—Representing Boredom

Whenever the palm is in a cupped position and placed directly under the chin with the fingers running alongside the face and the elbow used as a brace for support, this is a good indicator that a person is becoming bored or uninterested. The curled fingers may also be seen in front of the chin covering part of the lips. It is almost as if the person is trying to prop their head up to keep from falling asleep. However, it is very important to take note of what the eyes are doing at the same time. Observe if they are looking at the speaker, at the floor, an item on the table or desk, or seem to be staring off into space and seem as though they are distracted or in a daze.

This sign of boredom is even more pronounced and obvious when both hands are cupped under the chin with the elbows used to support and brace the head from lowering even further. The key is to recognize what position their hand was in when the conversation first started as well as how intent their eye gaze was towards the person talking. If the thumb and accompanying fingers are relaxed and showing interest, and then they move from that position demonstrating "light support" to a position with the head now needing assistance from the palm to hold it steady, the conversation has more than likely taken a turn, and your listener is being sidetracked by other thoughts. Seek the opportunity to change the topic and allow the other person to speak to get them to move their hand from under their chin, as they will not be able to talk comfortably as long as their palm is bracing and being supported under their jawline and chin.

The Shoulders

The shoulders help us determine whether a person feels confident or secure with their response. Typically, when we display a shrug of both shoulders in an upward motion in conjunction with open hands with upward-facing palms, this indicates that we do not have the answer to what we are saying or what was asked.

The shrugging motion with the open palms suggests that I am empty-handed or clueless on the subject at hand and have nothing to offer. An additional movement often seen with this display is the shaking of the head in a side-to-side motion, indicating "no."

The shrug of a single shoulder will suggest a guess or an approximation of something, but there is still uncertainty in the answer or statement. An example of this could be if someone asks you if you were at an event the night prior, and you answer yes. If they then ask how many people were there and you are not sure, you may respond with "I don't know, maybe thirty or forty?" while performing the single shoulder shrug along with the open palm gesture on the side of the shoulder that is shrugging.

Another important feature of the shoulders is as a means to try to protect the body. When a person is feeling fear or the need to protect themself from imminent danger, the head will attempt to shrink (or turtle itself) in between the shoulders to hide.

Also, as the head moves downward and the shoulders move upward, the hands will usually move to protect the face, with the palms facing out to shield oneself from harm. This motion may also be seen in conjunction with the facial expression of fear.

The Hands

The hands are a significant part of the body that assists us in communicating with people. They are considered to be illustrators or guides as they give direction and balance to our conversations. For individuals who are deaf, the hands provide the primary focus of the words, in conjunction with facial expressions, when using sign language.

Military groups also use hand signals and gestures, as do police department special operations units, to assist in silent communication during tactical operations. When training animals such as K-9s, trainers may also incorporate hand movements and signals to distinguish specific commands in conjunction with their voices.

When we meet someone for the first time, our hands relay important information to the person we are encountering. A friendly wave displaying an open hand demonstrates that one may be open for conversation and is potentially known to the person they are waving to.

Within the law enforcement community, as well as in general society, hands that are not visible may be viewed as a threat as the individual may possess a weapon or be concealing something they should not have or that could harm us. Open hands demonstrate to others that "I am friendly" or "I'm empty-handed and do not have anything to hide." When a person displays open hands, they do not pose an immediate threat and are viewed as  more friendly, believable, or approachable than those whose hands are not as visible.

The Handshake

As a part of meet and greets, the handshake assists in providing further information about the person one encounters. For centuries, a handshake has been a form of sealing the deal in negotiations as a form of trust. It is  also the first form of allowing someone to invade our personal space. While a handshake is not the sole indicator of an individual's overall personality, the following examples should aid in gauging this when meeting someone for the first time, especially when attempting to make a good impression.

A soft, loose handshake can be viewed as weak, uncertain, or lacking confidence. Negotiating or performing a business deal with this type of handshake could pose a potential problem. The weak shaker could be seen as a pushover and taken advantage of during the transaction.

A firm, level handshake represents a level of equality and balance between two individuals. It shows mutuality between the people shaking hands, that neither is viewed as higher than the other. From a personal or professional

stance, it shows that we are meeting on level ground, and I respect you just as much as you respect me.

 A strong, overpowering handshake can indicate one is attempting to display dominance or control. Besides being painful and overbearing, a vise grip of a handshake could also be interpreted as rude. After all, who wants to meet someone, shake hands, and have to deal with shielding pain from them during the next few moments of interaction?

Three Handshake Variations—Palm Down, Palm Up, and Parallel

In addition to differing handshake strength and firmness, people may also adopt one of the following three handshake variations: palm down, palm up, or the parallel or neutral handshake. Each of these handshakes exhibits different levels of submissiveness, equality, and superiority. As a result, your handshake can set the tone or mood of the conversation.

Palm Down

When a person approaches you to shake hands with their palm down, this is demonstrative of a dominant handshake. The individual is sending a subconscious message that they are in charge. This handshake comes from up high and leaves no option for the other person to equally hold their hand in the same way to complete the handshake.

Palm Up

When someone approaches you to shake hands with their palm facing up toward the ceiling, they are giving you the high ground and accepting the low ground. This handshake exhibits submission and gives the impression that "I am at your service, and it is my pleasure to meet you."

When making physical connections with others with our palms facing upward, we are giving them the upper hand. When you see pictures of individuals bowing down or kissing the hand or ring of those associated with authority or royalty, note that their palm is facing up while the palm of the person they are showing respect to is facing down.

Parallel

When being greeted with the hand in a parallel or side-by-side position without angling, both parties are demonstrating equality. This is representative that each person shaking hands has respect for the other, they are meeting on "level" ground, and neither is more important than the other. In a perfect world, we would hope that all levels of interactions would begin and end with neutral handshakes as this is usually the only form of physical touch, other than perhaps a hug, in which we allow strangers to get close to us.

Steepling of the Hands

Steepling of the hands is a display of confidence and indicates authority. This position is expressed with the hands parallel to each other and resembles that of prayer, with the exception of the hands being  opened and widened at the base. The fingertips will be in contact with each other, and the hands will form a diamond or possibly a triangle shape within the opening.

Often, this display is seen in meetings when those in a position of power are in thought concerning what they may be seeing or hearing. What is unique in this steeple pose is that it can be used in various positions. It may be seen just in front of the face near the base of the nose and mouth, resting on a tabletop or desk with the tips of the fingers pointing outward, or near the waistline while standing.

In the media, news briefings, and television interviews, this sign can readily be seen from political figures, business owners, and other people in positions of power when giving speeches or standing with others.

It should be noted that this display may be somewhat intimidating to others, especially if the points of the fingertips are aimed directly at them when statements are made. No one wants to feel as though they are being targeted, and direct finger-pointing can come across as overly assertive and accusatory. If using this pose while speaking, keep the fingertips pointed downward or close to the body rather than pushing or driving them outward toward your audience.

Fists

When hands become balled into fists, this demonstrates a strong level of emotion that is producing adrenaline. The initial appearance of fists can be viewed as a signal of potential danger.

However, depending on the height of the hands and the expression displayed, it could also be a sign of extreme happiness or joy. Typically, the higher the hands are raised, the more excitement and a sense of pride are displayed, as seen when someone wins a competition or when a referee raises the winner's hand, indicating their victory. This energetic balled fist raised high could be the result of an increase of dopamine running through the body, indicating a job well done.

When extreme happiness is demonstrated, a sense of pride may also be visibly present with the chin or head being raised higher than its normal resting position in conjunction with a smile.

On the other hand, when the hands are held low, tight, and below the waistline, near the sides, or near the chest level, this could be viewed as a sign of defense or preparation for battle. It also correlates to behavior associated with anger as well as danger. Because of this, one should be vigilant and highly observant and watch for micro and macro expressions that may be produced simultaneously in conjunction with the hands.

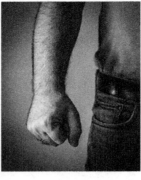

Fidgeting of the Hands

Fidgeting or twitchy hand movements are typical of an individual's nervousness or anxiety. These nonverbal motions are often seen with the hands and feet and may be heightened among people with social anxiety issues. Often, the person creating these movements with their hands may not be consciously aware of doing them. However, it may be readily obvious to others. The fidgeting may become a distraction depending on how frequent and intense the motion is.

About eleven years into my career, I was fortunate to be assigned to our training unit. I was responsible for training new cadets to the agency, creating lesson plans, and facilitating training needs for our members across the state. I remember my unit being requested to create a train-the-trainer course for our civilian counterparts that were going to start teaching members for some of their entry-level classes. We were a relatively small unit, so at times we would have to reach out to members from the field for additional support.

As my coworker and I began to develop this lesson plan, it was quite fun and exciting. I'll never forget watching my coworker in front of the class of potential trainers once the course was done, delivering his portion of the material. While he had been an instructor longer than I had, it was interesting to note that at the onset of the courses he taught he was always a bit nervous, and it showed in his hands. I remember one particular day when he started teaching while holding an ink pen that clicked to open and close. As he spoke to the audience, I noticed the click . . . click . . . click sound. The hand holding the pen was concealed by his opposite hand in front of him. The more nervous he became, the faster the clicks sounded. Within a matter of seconds, it sounded as though a sewing machine was running in the background. Of course, during times when it was necessary to point or illustrate specific movements, the sound stopped, but it would soon begin again. During one of the breaks, I pulled him to the side and told him to give me the pen, as I was sure the noise was distracting to the class since I could hear it from the rear of the room. He replied that he gets nervous and has to do something with his hands. Afterward, he got a paper clip and began manipulating it to ease his discomfort while standing in the front of the room. Later, I would occasionally joke with him and tell him that by the time he finished playing with the paper clip, it looked like he was doing some sort of origami with his hands.

Those who are aware of their nervous behavior may try to hide their hands from public view to conceal their actions. Also, some individuals may experience physiological reactions of sweating on their fingertips and palms, causing them to wipe or rub them on their pants and even place them inside their pockets to keep them as dry as possible. This is similar to the way that some athletes use dirt to dry their hands or gymnasts use chalk to clear any moisture or perspiration before performing to prevent mishaps.

The Legs

Crossing the legs while sitting can display a variety of emotional states and indicate an individual's confidence and comfort level. When individuals (namely males) sit with their legs spread apart, they are demonstrating comfort and confidence, as well as establishing a level of territory.

As they take up space, this is a position of dominance and may prevent others from approaching them with ease. This may be displayed when sitting on a bus, park bench, or any area shared by others when individuals are making the statement they are not willing to share or are claiming a particular domain of territory.

When males are sitting with their upper torso upright or they are relaxed, leaning backward while seated with their legs crossed in the figure four position, this can also be viewed as a level of confidence as more space is being taken up and the legs are still open, exposing one's private parts. Most people will never position themselves to expose their private parts unless they have an extreme level of comfort or confidence. Some males will sit this way merely for comfort when waiting in a lobby or even during face-to-face interviews. Be mindful of the leg crossing in a figure four position as it can also represent guarding oneself, as the bent leg can be used as a barrier separating one from another. This can sometimes be observed if something being talked about causes a person to feel uncomfortable, resistant, or defensive, and the leg moves from a neutral position in front to the figure four position. When discomfort or a level of stubbornness is present, one or both of the hands may hold the bent leg in place by the ankle or by the shin area to lock it securely and maintain the position. Context is always key when movements are made as one movement alone doesn't signify an exact interpretation of what is occurring. Movements and gestures must be measured on levels of congruency with verbal communication or the atmosphere where a person is located.

When the legs are close together without being crossed, this may indicate discomfort and a lack of confidence as it is a closed position shielding the private parts of the body. However, one must be mindful that with women, the legs will usually protect the private parts of their body, but the crossing of the legs in conjunction with their posture helps determine confidence level and possible discomfort.

As shown in both photos, these women would not sit in a way that exposes the private parts of their bodies since they are dressed in skirts. However, in each of the images, these women have their torsos in upright positions while leaning slightly forward, showing engagement, with their hands relaxed just below their chins, which demonstrates a level of confidence and illustrates that a person may be highly knowledgeable or genuinely interested in what is being stated. Their hands on their legs are also open with the fingers relaxed and without tension or rigidity. Their body language suggests that someone or something has their undivided attention, their eyes are focused on the object of that attention, and they are self-assured in their abilities.

In the photo above, the female is also seated in an upright position, but several areas of incongruency illustrate discomfort. Starting from the floor and moving upward, the feet do not show a sense of alignment as they are turned inward and facing each other, which provides an indicator of awkwardness.

While her upper legs are closed to prevent exposing her private parts, the lower legs, beginning at the knees and downward to the feet, are open and do not appear to be relaxed. The right hand on top of her legs is balled up in a fist, which may indicate some form of tension, stress, or anxiety. The left hand is being held close to the face near the mouth and also exhibits rigidness, which could be due to a sense of stress or anxiety. The left hand being near the mouth may indicate some emotional response to fear or nervousness as this individual may decide to bite her nails or cover her mouth in disbelief.

Both arms are placed close to the body, indicating a sense of being guarded to protect oneself. The left shoulder also demonstrates a bit of tension as it is higher than the right shoulder rather than being symmetrical and even. This gives the appearance that the head is trying to hide and shrink downward in between the shoulders.

Finally, the head is turned sideways and the eyes are looking at something, potentially indicating an overall sense of awkwardness. If more confidence traits were displayed as in the other photos, the head and chin would be more upright and frontal, indicating pride to challenge the situation or individual "head-on," and the hands would be more relaxed.

The Feet

The feet are great indicators in monitoring someone's body language during a conversation, regardless of whether the individual is sitting

or standing. Typically, our toes always point in the direction that we wish to travel. This makes sense because we don't want to walk in the wrong direction.

When speaking to someone, we want to give them our undivided attention, and because the body is symmetrically aligned, it would be awkward to see the feet shifted in any direction other than toward the person we are speaking with. If speaking with more than one person (such as standing with two others in a triangle position), we could see one of a person's feet pointing at the person to their left and the other at the person to their right. This would create balance and show equality among all parties involved. However, if someone's feet are shifted toward one individual in a multi-person conversation, it would be apparent that is where their focus and attention are directed.

When a person is ready to leave a discussion, their feet will often begin to shuffle and shift toward the direction in which they are ready to go, even though the shoulders and upper torso may be directed toward the person with whom they are speaking.

Mirroring

The mirroring technique is based on the idea that when an individual looks in a mirror, they see a reflection of themselves. As they move in the mirror, their reflection will also change.

In an interview session, sales meeting, or general conversation, this is a positive sign to look for when speaking to someone. Generally, as people talk to each other and become relaxed and comfortable, one of the individuals will begin to position themselves as if they are the mirror image of the person to whom they are speaking.

For example, suppose I am speaking to a person sitting in a chair, and I place my right arm on the back of the chair and bring my knees and torso toward the person I am speaking with. If the conversation remains interesting, the other party may reciprocate and mirror my actions but in the opposite direction with their arms and legs facing me.

Most people are not consciously aware they are performing this action, as it is a subconscious behavior that occurs without having to think about it. It is indicative of a person liking what they see or hear and wishing to be like the other person; hence, the word mirroring.

In sales meetings, job interviews, or getting to know someone on a personal or dating level, mirroring can demonstrate a positive connection with the other person. While doing repetitive movements, your attention is directed to them, and some level of rapport has definitely been established.

One must be mindful that if this technique of rapport building and maintaining interest is being done purposely, it is essential to avoid being obvious that you are mimicking the other person, as this can be viewed as disrespectful and cause immediate discord between the individuals involved.

Facial Zones/Gazes

When meeting someone for the first time or even during social, personal, and professional interactions, one must be mindful of how they present themselves and where they place their focus of attention.

Regardless of where the interaction occurs, eye contact plays an important part in nonverbal communication, as does the ability to remain focused.

When looking at others to communicate with them, there are three zones to be mindful of; these are the power gaze, social gaze, and intimate gaze. We will look at these further on the following pages.

The power gaze is typically used when an individual establishes a level of power by directing their view higher than eye level during a conversation. This gaze starts at eye level and goes upward toward the forehead area. It displays a level of authority, confidence, or dominance as they are not looking directly eye to eye with the other person, although it may seem as if they are.

Many organizational leaders may use a power gaze when providing instruction or direction to someone. This may also exhibit confidence in oneself that they are highly aware of what they mean to say. The power gaze may seem too direct and intimidating to some if the speaker's eyes do not move to other areas. As a result, the person being spoken to may shift their gaze away from the speaker.

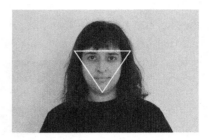

The social gaze is directed at the entirety of the face, in a triangular area beginning with the eyes and extending down to the mouth. It shows that one is engaged with all aspects of the other person and is focusing on them as they speak.

As the eyes maintain focus within this zone, it shows a level of connection between the speakers as they are illustrating they are paying attention. This will typically be seen during many of our daily interactions with people as it keeps conversations professional and shows a level of trust, equality, and respect for each party.

The intimate gaze is an extension of the social gaze as it also begins with the eyes, but it extends down to just below the neck area. It shows that one is interested in more than just the facial area and may wish to have a more intimate form of relationship. The eyes are traveling outside the normal boundaries, which may cause some to become uncomfortable if caught staring repeatedly during a conversation.

Ultimately, one must be careful and self-aware of which gaze they are using and how it may be interpreted. Some may use these gazes to be persuasive, to be perceived as interested, attracted, threatening, or intimidating, or to express some form of dominance.

It should also be noted that research has suggested that gazes in particular settings are used until they accomplish one's tasks, goals, or motives. With this in mind, self-awareness is of the utmost importance to ensure the information being sent to others is interpreted correctly.

Power Posing and Adjusting for Comfort

Body language gestures and displays are great indicators of how a person feels as well as what they are thinking. Amy Cuddy, an American social psychologist, did a TED talk explaining how high-power poses can shape us and increase our confidence while decreasing our stress levels. The purpose of these poses is to help empower the person using them by increasing their testosterone to boost their morale in a variety of circumstances. When we observe superheroes or people pos-  ing for photos who want to demonstrate strength, we notice how they take up space and spread their arms or legs, raise their head, or stick their chest out to express confidence and a lack of fear. Even when we request that someone show us their brave or confident pose, such as with their hands on their hips, we don't see the vulnerable areas of the body being concealed. One would think that since these poses are open and expose more target areas, people would refrain from showing this side of themselves to prevent injury or harm. However, power poses are not of long duration but just enough to increase our feeling of confidence and show others (if needed) that we are strong and lack fear.

 The equilateral triangle is one of the strongest shapes because of the angles it possesses. It is no surprise that because of its stability, rigidness, and power, it is used in construction for buildings and other structures. Pyramids are well known for their structurally sound base as well as their triangle sides and ability to stand the test of time. The sides of a triangle, no matter which of the various types, all create a balance with the angles they make, which gives structures support for withstanding weight and pressure. As a firearms instructor, throughout the years I've noticed a variety of shooting positions used by officers on the firing range. Quite often, one can identify stronger and weaker shooters merely by the firing stance they choose. Shooters that display stances with a good base platform and comfort are typically better shooters than those who appear narrow and awkward. Stronger shooters have an even level of balance that is reflected in all parts of the body, starting with how straight they keep their head, how relaxed the shoulders are, the straightness or bending in the arms and elbows, and the positioning of how they grip their handgun or rifle, all the way down to the bending of the knees and the spacing between their feet. For skilled and advanced shooters, I've come to realize the power in their body positions and their relationships to triangles. These individuals create angles via the joints and structure of their bodies that visually illustrate a variety of triangles. This provides a level of comfort and stability when shooting that allows them to breathe, concentrate, and maintain their position for a prolonged period of time without tiring easily.

When shooters are making mistakes, oftentimes it's due to a lack of training on how to stand with comfort, how to hold and manipulate their weapon, how to breathe, and how to align their sights properly with the target. Before novices are allowed to shoot, one of the best things they can do is practice how to stand and draw their weapon. As I train others on the range, one of the most important things I help them understand is how to be comfortable. After that is done, we work on postures that suit them. I have seen over the years that standing with a stable base and triangle formation from the feet up to the head offers the most support and facilitates the best shooting. This observation has strengthened my belief in poses in conjunction with levels of comfort as it enhances confidence in one's abilities.

A short while ago, I attended some training at a conference, and we talked about power posing and its effects on the body as well as the appearance it presents to others. To demonstrate this, we decided to do a practical exercise. We all went outside in the hotel lobby area and walked down the corridor to show two separate poses. The first was to walk with our heads down and shoulders forward, indicating low confidence and power, and the second was to walk back with our chins up slightly higher than level and our shoulders back.

We took up a good majority of the hallway area as other guests traveled up and down the corridor and had to pass by us to get to their destinations. I noticed that about 85 to 90 percent of the people that passed by us would make themselves smaller as they walked into our space. They would first lower their chins before getting within several feet of us and then cause their bodies to somewhat shrink by lowering their heads in between their shoulders. They also looked down toward the floor and slightly to the sides to ensure they did not touch anyone. Many of them would slightly speed up their pace to get through the commotion, saying "Excuse me" as they passed through our mini crowd. Ultimately, it was obvious that they were being polite and trying not to disrupt our experiment, but it was also clear they did not want to bring any unnecessary attention to themselves. Their body language exhibited slight intimidation even though there was no need for it. These patrons were merely trying to pass by without interrupting us and in doing so, attempted to make themselves less visible to avoid creating a disturbance or distraction.

However, the other 10 to 15 percent of individuals would come through our crowd with the same swagger and pace they had before entering our workspace. Their heads and chin levels remained at a moderate height, their pace did not slow or speed up, and our presence did not affect them one way or the other. Their confidence levels were not impacted, and their ability to walk upright was not altered in any way. As they walked through the area, they were not trying to be rude, but they also did not show any indicators of fear or intimidation. It was interesting to see that many of them were on a mission, and their vision was focused on what was in front of them as they didn't even seem interested in what we were doing.

When it comes to body language and the movements and gestures we make, a great portion of it stems from our confidence. Confidence is all about one's true sense of self and how comfortable they feel performing a task. There is a level of trust in themselves that may rise or fall depending on the circumstances in front of them. At times, it is obvious how confident some people are in comparison to those who have doubt. Having a conscious level of self-awareness based on our abilities should be our cue to power pose or put ourselves in positions that will allow us to relax and adjust for comfort. If you are someone that does not feel comfortable in many situations, I would suggest first working on small goals of seeing yourself being successful in what you want to achieve. A positive mindset is key in having the self-esteem to move forward in what holds us back. Acknowledging that you are not perfect is a huge step of progress even though we at times compare ourselves to others. Be yourself and take your time, and the success will come.

Chapter Eight

UNDERSTANDING COMBINATIONS

One Thing ≠ Everything

When attempting to read, monitor, or examine an individual, it is extremely important to recognize and understand that one specific sign in their body language does not mean deception. In other words, one sign does not always mean what a person thinks it does. Without being there in the moment and truly understanding what may or may not have taken place, it would be almost impossible to have a credible opinion without a great visualization or illustration of how the action or movement occurred. While micro expressions are emotional representations, when coupled with body language, they provide a reliable source of information with a higher probability of certainty as opposed to guessing or assuming.

In theory, the purpose of combinations is to have several options to solve an equation, as there is more than one way of coming up with the same answer or conclusion. Depending on the circumstances, the order of events is not as important as the outcome. In terms of cooking, the method of how ingredients are added and mixed together is important to ensure taste, texture, and other requirements are met before being able to move forward. However, in speaking with people, the same concept does not apply. It doesn't matter if a hand begins to sweat or a person inhales deeply or their foot begins to tap first when nervous, as their body mechanics may respond differently each time they are under stress. People will react and respond how they see fit when under stress just as when relaxed. There is no guideline that one must cross their leg when being guarded or show a micro expression when trying to shield an emotion.

Throughout our lives, we hear many ideas, myths, or theories about specific movements of the body and their alleged interpretations. Unfortunately, several of these theories have been disproven through research. As an individual, it is recommended to do your own research to ensure that your beliefs are true and accurate. Once you have more facts in front of you to evaluate, these bits and pieces of information should assist in making a more credible determination rather than an uninformed assumption.

Here are a couple of scenarios and theories as food for thought:

Scenario #1

An individual wakes up in the morning and looks outside their window. The sun is shining, and the birds are chirping. On the surface, it appears the day will be warm and sunny. They get dressed in a T-shirt and shorts and head out to enjoy a nice jog at the park. While at the park, the runner is shielded by trees as they run in bits and pieces of sunlight and shade. Out of nowhere, a dark cloud enters the area and a downpour begins, soaking the runner.

Just because the sun shines in the morning doesn't mean there will not be rain or thunder later in the day. As we all know, the weather can change with little to no notice. However, if the sun begins to fade and dark clouds appear along with thunder and lightning and wind gusts, there is a good chance that a storm will soon occur.

Just as the shift from one variance of weather to another will present itself in the clouds, wind, thunder, drizzle, etc., so can an individual when being questioned about specifics during conversations in which they may begin to feel uncomfortable. This may also be reflected in the tone, pitch, and rate of speed of their verbal responses. Changes in temperature in the atmosphere (sunny to shady, hot to cold, dry to wet) as well as in an individual (such as sweating, blood flow to the face, appearing pale or reddening) will be noticeable almost instantly as they occur. Take note of these while speaking or monitoring conversations, as they are great indicators that something has been triggered in the body.

Scenario 2

A participant is sitting in the front row of an audience listening to a guest speaker at a conference for work. The speaker begins to talk about salary increases and modifying the company's organization chart. The participant leans back in their seat and crosses their arms across their body for the duration of the presentation. As soon as the guest speaker completes the presentation, the participant uncrosses their arms, gives the presenter a standing ovation, and acknowledges a job well done, as it was one of the best ideas they have heard for the company in a long time.

Just because someone crosses their arms, it is not a definitive sign that they are guarded or upset. This alone does not prove that a person is lying or being deceptive. This is probably one of the biggest misconceptions and myths in the body language community. It could be that the person is cold or putting themselves in a position to relax or self-soothe.

However, if coupled with inhaling and exhaling deeply along with negative facial expressions, it could be reasoned that the individual is more than likely showing a potential form of frustration. Also, one would want to determine whether the shoulders are in a relaxed position, being held low with the arms crossed just below chest level, or if they are being held in an upright position where they appear to be pulled upward toward the ears with the arms slightly higher.

Scenario #3

Two customers are standing in line at a local grocery store, and a woman looks over her shoulder and briefly smiles at a man standing behind her. She says hello, and within a few moments, the two engage in small talk about the concert coming to town in the next few weeks while waiting on the cashier. The two seem to have a common interest in music groups, as determined through their brief interaction. Before she leaves, the gentleman invites her out on a date to the concert, and the woman politely declines and says she is in a relationship. Still, she appreciates the conversation they had while they waited in line.

When an individual smiles at another, does it mean they like them in an intimate manner? Smiling at someone does not by itself prove one is attracted to another person. In business opportunities and the basics of rapport building, smiling at others is suggested as a way to appear nonthreatening and build trust. Far too often, individuals may misinterpret innocent conversations and smiles being exchanged as flirting.

However, suppose the opportunity presents itself, and she seems to be getting closer within his intimate zone and applying simple grooming or soft touching tactics. In that case, this may indicate that she feels extremely comfortable with him and may want to get to know him on a deeper or more personal level. The situation should be examined to determine how long they remain in the intimate zone to establish their comfort level and what they say and do while in close proximity to check for congruency and avoid making a judgment error.

Scenario #4

A couple of colleagues are in the company break room talking about an upcoming meeting. During the conversation, a fellow employee enters and sneezes, then immediately goes to blow their nose. One of the colleagues offers some over-the-counter medication to help with that sneeze. The coworker thanks them but mentions that another coworker had sprayed some air freshener moments before and they walked into the mist, which caused a mild irritation.

A sneeze alone doesn't mean a person is becoming ill. Neither does two sneezes back-to-back. This could merely be an indication that a person was exposed to some dust in the atmosphere, or they may have seasonal allergies that were temporarily triggered.

However, if accompanied by coughing, a runny nose, and body aches, it could be an indicator that they are in the early stages of becoming ill. Observing these indicators gives one something to recall with credibility and use to further establish a belief that a person is ill.

The biggest key in making these determinations is to monitor the individual, watch for consistency in their actions, and search for additional signs that accompany the other traits being shown.

Scenario #5

A parent is taking their child to school in the morning. As they approach the school zone, the crossing guard blows their whistle and enters the roadway commanding traffic to stop from both directions. Due to inattention, a driver does not see the crossing guard in the middle of the roadway until the last minute. The crossing guard uses their hand and voice to emphasize to the driver to stop their vehicle. Realizing the urgency, the driver comes to a stop and waves their hand to the crossing guard in return to show acknowledgment, recognition, understanding, and an apology.

When a person displays their hand with five fingers, are they asking for five of something, or are they signifying that someone must stop? Are the fingers distanced apart and relaxed, or are they tense and aligned? Could they be waving at someone they know? And what is the rest of the body saying? Is their facial expression demonstrative of anger, or is it relaxed?

Tense or rigid hands and fingers usually indicate signs of being authoritative, aggressive, defensive, or under some form of stress. We may often see this behavior when someone is arguing with another and demanding something. Loose or open hands and fingers typically demonstrate that one is open, calm, nonthreatening, and friendly and does not present any danger.

The Takeaway

In attempting to verify an emotion or specific state of being, I would strongly recommend that you confirm at least three indicators before prejudging or assuming you are correct. Keep in mind that these three emotional signs may not erupt all at once. In other words, they may not occur back-to-back within a few seconds like a domino effect. However, through further questioning and observing the issue or initial cause (stimulus) for the behavior and action, one should be able to create follow-ups (additional questions) to confirm or dispel the assumption they made based off one indicator.

One needs to have more of a baseline (accurate interpretation under normal or non-stressful circumstances) of the person being observed or spoken to before making the judgment that they are being deceitful. Once the entire situation can be viewed in its totality, a practitioner of body language and micro expressions should be able to come to an educated and well-informed conclusion based on facts rather than suspicions or a hunch.

Do not fall victim to believing that one gesture alone constitutes a full explanation of what something is or is not. While you may be onto something with your initial suspicion, it should be well-established and validated to strengthen your conclusion. The ability to articulate your reasoning always confirms your credibility, and being honest when uncertain and replying that you do not have an answer or simply do not know is much better than wildly guessing.

Congratulations! Now that you have gained an understanding of the foundational concepts for learning body language and micro expressions as well as the tools needed to learn and be successful, I welcome you to continue on your path as we delve into what the body is saying and how to do your part to further aid you and cause your superpowers to flourish.

Chapter Nine

HOW TO SEE WHAT THE BODY IS SAYING

If you don't have a vision, you're going to be stuck in what you know. And the only thing you know is what you've already seen.
~ IYANLA VANZANT

The fear of the unknown may hinder some from moving forward, but it may also cause others to seek further insight to better understand what could possibly be. Remaining stagnant is one of the greatest ways to prevent one from growing or developing a skill. I firmly believe that if one can imagine something, the possibility of it becoming a reality cannot be too far from reach. Unfortunately, we sometimes keep our minds trapped in cages that we can see out of. When the door is opened, it becomes apparent that we could have stepped out at any time, but we felt as though we were restricted. In other words, many of our restrictions and limiting beliefs are due to our mindset.

Once I began performing investigations and had daily face-to-face interactions with people, being proficient in distinguishing fact from fiction was an absolute necessity. While I had the desire to believe that suspects, victims, and witnesses were always truthful, the harsh reality was that this was not always the case. Not long after I was selected to go to polygraph school, I was asked to provide insight to our new recruits on some aspects of interviewing and interrogation techniques. While creating an entire lesson plan from scratch, I sought out videos and information to provide and maintain interest for both the inexperienced and those who had experience interviewing others.

During my search, I discovered information concerning micro expressions of the face and their importance in concealing the emotions of the person displaying them. My curiosity was sparked, and I became highly intrigued by the work of Dr. Paul Ekman. While I had previously learned about the brain, its functions, and how it relates to specific systems in the body when nervousness, fear, and apprehension are involved, I had not yet been introduced to the face and the information it holds and tries to prevent others from seeing. I furthered my research on body language gestures and cues and found even more information to add to my tool belt.

I thought back to times during interviews when I did not get a confession but had a strong feeling of the person's guilt and could not articulate why. Those times made me feel as though I was a failure and put a sense of fear within me. I realized I lacked the SKILL in areas that were necessary to adequately do my job. After learning more about micro expressions and body language recognition, I felt I would be better equipped to encounter any situation with more confidence, but I needed to practice analyzing reality-based techniques to get the results I desired. Hence, I had to do my **PART** (**P**ractice **A**nalyzing **R**eality-based **T**echniques) and finally step out of my cage as I now had a new mindset to help move me forward.

Practice—the action of "training or refining" one's skills and abilities.

Practice is the first step in getting better in any and all aspects of life. Practice is more or less an upgrade of trying. Anyone can "try" something, but to practice requires will and determination. If you look at any professional athlete, whether in the Olympics, basketball, football, boxing, soccer, swimming, tennis, etc., they will often attribute their success to hard work and determination. The training they had to perform was neither easy nor an overnight accomplishment.

To improve at any task, some level of repetition to refine and enhance the skill will have to occur. There will frequently be failures throughout our lives, but we should not let that discourage us from getting better. Failure is a sign that should be associated with trying. If one is not failing, they are either not trying, remaining stagnant in their current position, or performing exceedingly well at whatever they do. Weightlifters often work their muscles to the point of failure to break them down and cause them to get stronger and larger over time. Pushing them to the limit creates a long-term gain. Failure brings many individuals to a crossroads or potential dead end, which ultimately causes them to reevaluate their plans and goals. Failure also typically provides some lesson that will be valuable in attempting to redo an earlier task.

When practicing body language and micro expression recognition, practice may not make one an expert overnight. Still, it will produce better accuracy in determining truth from deception and recognizing emotions in people we encounter daily. The key is to first start learning and push oneself daily to refine the skills that already exist within us and bring them to a better light to see more clearly than ever.

Analyzing—the action of "scrutinizing or critically examining" an object or situation.

The ability to analyze anything requires a trained eye. The first part of analyzing is knowing what to look for and then monitoring the behavior or reactions. This action requires the looking and listening criteria based on the SKILL process (covered in an earlier chapter). Once the information observed is visually and possibly audibly processed, one must be able to scrutinize what they saw and then determine what it meant. This scrutiny aids in breaking down the details of expressions and body language, allowing us to articulate what we know rather than what we think.

The ability to analyze is twofold. As practitioners, we must be mindful and realize that just as we look at, listen to, and analyze others, the same may be done to us. The ability to analyze ourselves and be consciously aware of what we are doing and present in the moment may prove difficult at first. We must be cognizant that our expressions, movements, and emotions may cause others to react. For example, suppose I am giving someone a look of anger or showing confusion or some form of mistrust or judgment. In that case, they may become nervous and start to project those expressions during our interaction, which I may then believe to be signs of deception or anxiety.

Reality-based—the "actuality of being real, authentic, or unscripted."

Reality-based training is the closest alternative when actual circumstances to practice do not exist. This type of training, which is based on real-life situations, can be created with little to no expense.

For example, watching live television shows (award shows, news coverage, sports events, etc.) allows one to see authentic expressions based on questions and answers and other types of interaction. Also, reviewing prerecorded interview sessions on the internet or on talk shows enables one to see body language indicators that demonstrate comfort, relaxation, confusion, or anger. Creating mock interview sessions between two or more people that introduce questions designed to elicit specific responses offers no opportunity to rehearse the conversation and demands that role-players be engaged and interactive.

Within the military and law enforcement communities, reality-based training plays an integral role in their ability to perform their jobs in real life. These professions may use nonlethal, color-marking rounds for firearms training to indicate where or how someone is shooting. They may perform driver's training at high speeds to create a controlled stress-inducing environment to ensure they can function and control themselves and their vehicles with great accuracy under pressure.

Businesses and corporations will also utilize reality-based training in dealing with disgruntled employees or agitated customers to train their employees on the value of self-recognition to maintain control of themselves as well as recognize changes in the other individual's behavioral patterns.

Techniques—the "mode or manner" of how one approaches a situation or circumstance.

A technique is how one ultimately executes or carries out a particular task. It is based on practical skills learned and the way the individual uses them. The beauty of a technique is that everyone has their own way of doing things. For example, two painters may be able to paint a picture, but one may paint it in an upright position while the other paints it upside down. Either way is acceptable if the desired result is achieved. It doesn't matter if one of the painters took thirty minutes and the other took an hour. The outcome of the artwork was completed successfully.

In learning the concepts of micro expressions and body language, the technique and style of how one uses their skill are completely up to them. One may choose not to read micro expressions while another may rely heavily on them. Others may wish to use both micro expressions and body language to assist them during their interactions with others. Ultimately, there is no right or wrong way, as one must do what feels best for them. Having access to the face in some circumstances may prove advantageous if the body cannot readily be seen, or vice versa if the face is slightly covered and one can see more of the body. Understanding both of these areas allows one to adjust their technique of how to look for indicators involving emotions, truth, and deception.

The concepts presented in the previous chapters have provided information to enlighten you or enhance your understanding of nonverbal communication in a way you may not have ever imagined. Keep in mind the concepts will not be difficult to grasp if you stay committed, but be ready to try your newfound knowledge and put it to use. One of the most important things to remember in learning and practicing the skills contained in this book is that you are not forced to rush, and there is no deadline for completion. You can work at your own pace and apply the skills you possess as you see fit. Your progress will be measured based on the goals and objectives you set for yourself.

I challenge you to take your time, do your **PART**, and put the **SKILL** learned from this book to use in making your pursuit of learning micro expressions and body language an unforgettable journey. This book has started you on an introductory path or was perhaps a refresher of previous skills and working knowledge. Do not stop once you have completed it. Continue your path to learn more, as this is only the beginning of understanding human behavior and the methodology of how we communicate with one another.

Chapter Ten

PUTTING IT ALL TOGETHER

**Trust is congruence between what
you say and what you do.
~ PETER DRUCKER**

uccess is measured by the individual seeking a certain growth
or change level. Success for you may be different than for
another. One percent higher or lower, depending on the type of
achievement sought, can be viewed as a level of success. The overall
value here is that no one can diminish your success level unless you
allow them to. Quite often, I think we as individuals get fixated on seeing
a large amount of change to demonstrate a massive improvement. This
may be the overall desire for some, but having a lesser amount of change
does not disqualify one from being recognized as demonstrating some
level of accomplishment.

As we take a moment to reflect on whether the theories of body language
and micro expressions are beneficial in our lives, just think back to times
in your life when you have felt a certain way about someone else's words
or actions, and intuition was just not enough to determine whether they
were being truthful.

Reading and recognizing behaviors and expressions is a skill that anyone can master if they are willing to dedicate the time, energy, and effort. In the grand scheme of reading body language and interpreting facial expressions, one will recognize that there is no definitive way of determining truth from lies. Even throughout my years as a polygraph examiner, one specific instrument was not able to definitively distinguish truth from deception. Overall, it takes several areas of observation in conjunction with a conversation to interpret what one sees.

However, with practice, the ability to better understand and ask additional questions based on what is initially seen can lead to further questioning and observation. Then, reexamining what is being presented can lead to a more accurate determination of whether one's suspicions are accurate.

As human beings, we can do many things and possess numerous skills and gifts. Continued practice in any craft can lead to mastery of it. As we do anything regularly and with consistency, it becomes a part of us and it gets easier, perhaps even effortless. It may also become a habit. Think back to when you learned how to tie your shoes. At first you had to look at what you were doing, calculate, and go through the motions of how to pull and maneuver the strings through the holes; strings were overlapped right over left or left over right, a bow was created and tied, and eventually, it became common practice to put your shoes on and tie them without even looking at what you were doing. The practice of doing these actions daily created a habit, which was reinforced and embedded as muscle memory.

Another example would be learning to drive a car. When initially learning and finally in the driver's seat, many novice drivers are afraid to drive without both hands on the steering wheel. They will not look around to check their surroundings, nor will they perform frequent mirror checks or monitor their speed accurately, and they cannot do much more than concentrate on one or two things at a given time. Why is that? Because it is a new skill (in progress) that has not yet been mastered, the comfort and confidence level is very low, and the need to focus and pay attention to specifics is typically higher than average. However, after months and years of practice, many are able to drive with confidence as their skill level and abilities have increased. This is often seen as people drive and change the radio, talk on the phone, talk to others in the vehicle, and so on. The learned and repeated behavior becomes second nature and is done with little to no conscious effort or thought.

The same concept applies to learning micro expressions and interpreting body language. Many new to this skill will stare at the face waiting to see an expression or deeply analyze every single body movement and attempt to decode its meaning. However, with continued practice, one will be able to look at the body as a whole to determine facial expressions, minor body changes, and nuances with ease, in conjunction with analyzing what is being said by the person they are observing.

I think back to when I was first starting and was inexperienced in interviewing and interrogating people; there is no telling how much information and how many telltale signs passed right before my eyes. However, once I had taken some basic courses in interviewing and began watching suspects, victims, and witnesses get interviewed by other officers and investigators, I saw my colleagues making the same mistakes that I had in the past.

Over time, I gained more confidence and became more comfortable. My newfound skill set began to pay off, and interviewing sometimes appeared to get easier. I would share what I had learned with other investigators who were just as interested as I was. I continued to seek additional training to become the best at my craft, often at my own expense.

As I took various classes, I understood the information obtained was an opportunity to add another tool to my tool belt that could be used for specific occasions. While no two people are exactly the same, it was interesting to see the many ways that human beings are alike. The emotions we display and the ways we use illustrators, adapters, and nonverbal body language indicators are not significantly different.

Starting from ground zero, learning a new skill can initially seem difficult. However, one key to succeeding is to avoid becoming overwhelmed. Starting anything that one has never done before or stepping into unfamiliar territory should be treated just as a child learning to walk or ride a bike.

Some years ago, I started learning the kung fu martial art form of Wing Chun. My teacher, Sifu Brian Edwards, always told us to keep a notebook and write notes after each class, so we would have something to reference later. I am so grateful for his advice because it is unbelievable how much information we forget when we do not write things down, assuming we will remember them later. When I first started, I used to wonder why we would do one particular drill repeatedly throughout the class, which at times would seem like forever. I quickly realized it was for muscle memory, technique improvement, and building comfort while being under stress. The same methodology applies to learning this art of reading nonverbal communication.

Even though the newfound abilities will flow as natural reflexes over time, it is equally important to be aware of your own emotions, facial expressions, and body language when interacting with others. The ability to read others while lacking the ability to control oneself may not produce the successful results one expects. We must always be mindful that the reactions we display to others may cause them to react in a way that we feel is offensive when in fact, we are their trigger.

Failure to adapt and adjust to existing circumstances could cause the loss of a job during an interview, the end of a business deal, or problems in personal and professional relationships. The ultimate plan is to learn from any mistakes made and continue to push forward to be the best at whatever you intend to do.

For the next thirty days, I challenge you to begin your journey in doing your **PART** to put the information in this book to use. Create a four-week journal to track your notes for each week documenting what you see in others as well as yourself during daily interactions. Expect to experience frustration and miss subtle cues and gestures, but get back up and stay in the fight. I cannot stress enough the importance of practicing daily to increase your proficiency level. Do not hesitate to ask questions involving the unknown, and refuse to allow others to tell you that you won't succeed.

I recommend starting with the seven universal facial micro expressions. Review each one and study its traits. Practice performing these facial expressions yourself and feel the emotion created within you to better understand what you see displayed in someone else. Begin watching reality TV shows, news interviews with the general public, and documentaries with celebrities, as well as the people you interact with daily. Monitor these expressions with and without volume as no sound is necessary to observe them. If you want to take your skills to the next level, record yourself while watching movies or TV shows to see how *you* are responding to what you see and hear.

Once a greater level of comfort has been established in observing micro expressions, check the congruency of what the person says with the emotion you see displayed. If a person states they were scared to death, did they show any sign of fear? If someone indicates they are sad about doing something bad, are they contradicting themselves and showing some form of happiness? Being able to assess the spoken words in conjunction with the nonverbal cues displayed is a great tool in evaluating a person's authenticity in their emotions, as opposed to them just stating something that seems appropriate.

Next, move forward in your pursuit and watch for general signs of the body. Notice how people shake your hand or avoid shaking your hand upon meeting them. Observe how people use their hands as illustrators during conversation while also noting any lack of movement during specific conversations that would typically involve some form of activity. Be mindful of the different levels of proxemics as people shop in department stores and grocery store aisles. The familiarity of friends and family members will become more apparent over time compared with people meeting for the first time or simple casual encounters.

As you start to see the commonalities of how people are alike in so many ways, you will be better able to put it all together as you monitor micro expressions and body language for congruency. You will quickly be able to note anomalies and discrepancies in what was said and what was shown right before your eyes! Embrace what you see and attempt to follow up with questions when you observe areas that do not match to see if other emotions arise.

Remember during the process of learning that progress comes with time. If reading body language and micro expressions were super easy, everyone would be able to do it with little to no practice. Sifu Edwards used to say, "There are two types of martial artist—people who talk martial arts and people who do martial arts." I feel the same way about becoming a micro expression and body language practitioner. Some people talk about body language, and then there are practitioners who actually see and evaluate body language. My challenge for you is to decide which path you will take. Be the best at whichever you select, for there is no right or wrong answer.

Train your eyes, recognize your emotional self-awareness and mind, and be prepared for new levels of advancement within your personal and professional life. In return, pay your newfound skills forward and help someone else discover their own hidden superpowers. Let the sky be the limit in your pursuit of becoming an expert in whatever field you choose. Stay the course, and do not be afraid to share your experiences to show there is more than one way to see things when learning how to read others. It would be an honor to know that the information you have learned here was beneficial in growing the opportunities that await you.

I would love to hear your success stories, so feel free to connect and share with me as you grow and develop your skill set!

It's amazing what you'll see in others
when you know what to look for.
~ RODNEY SMITH

BIBLIOGRAPHY

Bambaeeroo, F., & Shokrpour, N. (2017). The impact of the teachers' nonverbal communication on success in teaching. *Journal of Advances in Medical Education & Professionalism*, 5(2), 51–59.

Bock, Kristin. (2022, February 15). *A nod to comedian Sarah Cooper.* Body Language Blueprints. https://bodylanguageblueprints. com/blog/a-nod-to-comedian-sarah-cooper/

Bond Jr., C. F., & DePaulo, B. M. (2006). Accuracy of deception judgments. *Personality and Social Psychology Review*, 10(3), 214–234.

Dispatch. (2013, January). *Did you know...* https://cops.usdoj.gov/ html/dispatch/01-2013/did-you-know.asp

Driver, J., & van Aalst, M. (2010). *You say more than you think: The 7-day plan for using the new body language to get what you want.* Crown Publishers.

Ekman, P. (2007). *Emotions revealed: recognizing faces and feelings to improve communication and emotional life.* OWL Books.

Elsesser, K. (2018, April 3). Power posing is back: Amy Cuddy successfully refutes criticism. *Forbes*. https://www.forbes.com/ sites/kimelsesser/2018/04/03/power-posing-is-back-amy-cuddy-successfully-refutes-criticism/?sh=388dbf7f3b8e

Fremont-Smith, K. (2022, March 9). *How to change your own contempt.* The Gottman Institute. https://www.gottman.com/blog/how-to-change-your-own-contempt/

Freud, S. (1953). A Case of Hysteria, Three Essays on Sexuality and Other Works. In *The standard edition of the complete psychological works of Sigmund Freud,* (Vol. VII, pp. 1–122). The Hogarth Press.

Glass, L. (2013). *The body language of liars: from little white lies to pathological deception—how to see through the fibs, frauds, and falsehoods people tell you every day.* Red Wheel/Weiser.

Haggard, E. A., & Isaacs, K. S. (1966). Micromomentary facial expressions as indicators of ego mechanisms in psychotherapy. In L. A. Gottschalk & A. H. Auerbach (Eds.), *Methods of research in psychotherapy* (pp. 154–165). Springer.

Hamilton, C. (2021, July 2). *Emotional powerhouse: The sacral chakra.* Midtown Yoga Studios. https://midtownyogastudios.com/blog/the-sacral-charka

Hans, A., & Hans, E. (2015). Kinesics, haptics and proxemics: Aspects of nonverbal communication. *IOSR Journal of Humanities and Social Science (IOSR-JHSS), 20*(2), 47–52.

Hartley, G., & Rouse, S. (2020). *Body language tactics* [Online]. Available at https://courses.bodylanguagetactics.com/enrollments

Hernandez, J., Paredes, P., Roseway, A., & Czerwinski, M. (2014, April). Under pressure: sensing stress of computer users. In *Proceedings of the SIGCHI conference on Human factors in computing systems* (pp. 51–60).

Hughes, C. (2020). *Six minute X-ray advanced behavior profiling course* [Online]. Available at https://chasehughes.com

Hurley, C. M. (2012). Do you see what I see? Learning to detect micro expressions of emotion. *Motivation and Emotion, 36*(3), 371–381.

Kleinke, C. L. (1986). Gaze and eye contact: A research review. *Psychological Bulletin, 100*(1), 78–100.

Kulaksız, E. (2015). To what extent does culture create language learning in terms of proxemics. *Procedia-Social and Behavioral Sciences, 199,* 695–703.

Levine, T. R., Kim, R. K., Sun Park, H., & Hughes, M. (2006). Deception detection accuracy is a predictable linear function of message veracity base-rate: A formal test of Park and Levine's probability model. *Communication Monographs, 73*(3), 243–260.

Ligia. (2023, August 25). *Why do Costa Ricans love invading your personal space?.* Costa Rica Travel Blog and Tips by Locals. https://exploretikizia.com/costa-ricans-love-invading-personal-space/

Lindberg, S. (2020, August 24). *What are chakras? Meaning, location, and how to unblock them.* Healthline. https://www.healthline.com/health/what-are-chakras#bottom-line

Murray, W. (2022, April 8). *Energy reading for beginners: What's really happening when the vibes are off.* Thriveworks. https://thriveworks.com/blog/energy-reading-vibes/

Navarro, J. (2018). *The dictionary of body language: A field guide to human behavior.* William Morrow Paperbacks.

Navarro, J., & Karlins, M. (2008). *What every body is saying.* HarperCollins Publishers.

Okazaki, S., Liu, J. F., Longworth, S. L., & Minn, J. Y. (2002). Asian American-White American differences in expressions of social anxiety: A replication and extension. *Cultural Diversity and Ethnic Minority Psychology, 8*(3), 234.

Pease, A. & Pease, B. (2006). *The definitive book of body language.* Bantam Books.

Prooyen, E. V. (2022, March 10). *This one thing is the biggest predictor of divorce.* The Gottman Institute.

Riggio, R. E., & Feldman, R. S. (2005). *Applications of nonverbal communication.* Psychology Press.

Stern, R. M., Ray, W. J., & Quigley, K. S. (2001). *Psychophysiological recording.* Oxford University Press.

Tewari, A. (2022, July 7). *700 affirmations to balance all 7 chakras.* Gratitude - The Life Blog. https://blog.gratefulness.me/chakra-affirmations/

Van Edwards, V. (2016, September 1). How body language can help your career. *Time.* https://time.com/4462658/body-language-tips/

Van Edwards, V. (2021, March 6). *20 leg body language cues to help you analyze any situation*. Science of People. https://www.scienceofpeople.com/leg-body-language/#:~:text=This%20is%20because%20crossing%20legs,re%20feeling%20submissive%20or%20defensive

Wezowski, P., & Wezowski, K. (2019). *Micro expressions training videos* [Online]. Available at https://microexpressionstrainingvideos.com/members/

Zorfass, N. (2022, July 13). *What are the 7 chakras and what do they each mean?* Speakeasy Inc. http://speakeasyinc.com/

ABOUT THE AUTHOR

R odney Smith is the owner and operator of Smith's Professional Services, LLC (dba Rodney Smith & Associates). He has spent over twenty years as a law enforcement officer and started his career as a patrol and traffic enforcement officer with the Fayetteville Police Department in Fayetteville, North Carolina.

A few years later, he transitioned to the NC DMV License & Theft Bureau as an inspector and became introduced to various specialized criminal and regulatory investigations. After working several years in the field, Rodney was transferred to his agency's training unit and assisted with its operations until being promoted to the rank of lieutenant. He returned to supervise, oversee, and assist members in the field.

Several years later, he was blessed once again and promoted to the rank of captain and returned to oversee the actions of the Training and Development Unit for all of the sworn law enforcement members within the Bureau across the state.

He holds several criminal justice certifications in the state of North Carolina as a general, firearms, driving, CPR, rapid deployment, and solo active shooter instructor, to name a few. Rodney has also been the lead interviewing techniques instructor for his agency's basic training academy for almost a decade. In addition, he has been trained to instruct forensic vehicle identification number (VIN) restoration with the use of acid for altered motor vehicle numbers. He is a Virginia School of Polygraph graduate in the study of psychophysiological detection of deception and conducts preemployment and criminal polygraphs for his department.

He has a Bachelor of Arts in Criminal Justice from Pembroke State University and a Master of Science in Criminal Justice Administration from North Carolina Wesleyan in Rocky Mount, North Carolina.

Rodney has taken several courses in interview and interrogation, statement analysis, body language, and micro expressions. He is a certified micro expressions and body language trainer with the Center for Body Language. He is also certified as a senior instructor with the Body Language Institute in Alexandria, Virginia, through Body Language Expert Janine Driver. He has been certified as a trainer with The Congruency Group through Body Language/Interview and Interrogation Expert Lena Sisco to instruct elicitation techniques. Rodney is also a certified hypnotist with the National Guild of Hypnotists, a certified iridologist, and a certified master face reader practitioner in Chinese face reading.

In 2020, he was given the opportunity to present a TED talk in Raleigh, North Carolina, titled "The Power of Communication and Body Language." During this presentation, he provided information regarding his "ABCs of Communication," which are Active Listening, Body Language, and Communication.

Rodney has been featured several times on CourtTV and provided information as a body language expert in many recent and ongoing court cases.

He is a member of several law enforcement and investigative organizations such as the International Association of Interviewers (IAI), American Association of Police Polygraphists (AAPP), NC Polygraph Association, ASIS, International Association of Law Enforcement

Firearms Instructors (IALEFI), and the International Association of Auto Theft Investigators (IAATI).

He also teaches as an adjunct criminal justice instructor with Fayetteville Technical Community College in Fayetteville, North Carolina, and NC Wesleyan College in Rocky Mount, North Carolina. In those institutions, he teaches Investigative Principles, Interview and Interrogation, Criminal Law, and Report Writing for our future criminal justice professionals.

He is a peer-reviewed author featured in Volume 1, Issue 1, July 2020 of *The Journal of Criminal Justice Professionals*, in which he wrote the paper "Law Enforcement Training: When Millennials Become Police Officers." He is also featured as a contributing author in the textbook *Policing in a Diverse Society: Another American Dilemma (2nd ed.)*, in which he wrote the chapter "Policing in a Diverse Society from an Officer's Perspective: Issues of Low Morale in the Workplace."

Rodney currently lives with his wife and is surrounded among his other family members in his hometown of Fayetteville, North Carolina. In his free time, he loves to watch movies, attend family gatherings, practice martial arts, continue learning and researching to expand his knowledge in various areas, and spend as much time as he can with his grandson.

Are you interested in learning more about
training and teachings from Rodney?

Contact Rodney Smith at:

www.therodneysmith.com

It's not hard if you know what you're doing.
~ RODNEY SMITH